Magical Paris

Over 100 Things to Do Across Paris

K. B. Oliver

Updated 2022

Monceau Publishing

Books and Resources by K. B. Oliver

Books

Magical Paris: Over 100 Things to Do Across Paris

A French Garden: The Loire Valley

Real French for Travelers

Resources

Real French for Travelers Complete Online Course

realfrenchfortravelers.com

(Find your discount code for the Complete Online Course in the Pronunciation and Language chapter!)

Oliver's France Website (for travel tips and ideas)

Free online mini-Course on French polite words and greetings on the website.

www.Oliversfrance.com

Introduction to the 2022 Update

Magical Paris: Over 100 Things to Do

Across Paris

The 2022 version is finally here! Last year, I set out to update Magical Paris, as I do every other year, but we were still deep into Covid. I quickly realized I had to postpone the update because there were too many museums and tourist sites closed or operating on reduced schedules, as well as many other restrictions.

Today, museums and tourist sites in Paris are again open with normal hours! Three years after the last update, what has changed? Hours are mostly the same as **pre-Covid**. Pricing has risen only slightly in most cases, or not at all. The primary change is that many places, though not all, still require showing a "pass sanitaire", or vaccine certificate. Most don't require masks anymore (take them just in case), and quite a few require reservations online. Check the places you'd like to go online before you leave. The upside of ordering online is you can be sure of having a spot and sometimes you can avoid waiting in line. Be sure to check any changing requirements for your airline and entering France right before you leave, since this changes often. Enjoy your trip!

K. B. Oliver

Traveling is back! Bon voyage!

Table of Contents

MAGICAL PARIS

Introduction

The last time you saw that movie that took place in Paris, you may have said to yourself, "That looks so charming and picturesque. I wonder if it's really like that."

And now it's your chance to actually *go* to Paris and see for yourself. I can tell you, after living in France for 13 years, that Paris really *is* like that and better. In fact, it's magical. Paris is a city where even ordinary residential streets seem to jump out of another century. Flower shops burst with color and variety, adorning the busy sidewalks. Cafés warmly draw you in. Cobblestones underfoot remind you that you're walking through history. It's no wonder that more people visit Paris, France, than any other tourist destination, year after year.

Maybe it's your second, third, or tenth visit. There's so much to see that you never get tired of this enchanted city.

If you're like most people, you have a few things that you *must* see when you get there. These may be the places that launch the first chapter of nearly all travel books. Many of these sites are clustered near the center of the city. Of course, you'll want to see all of these. Those that leap to mind are the Eiffel Tower, the Notre Dame Cathedral, the Louvre ...

Other visitors want all that, *plus much more*. They want to wander off the beaten track further out from the city center. They want to get lost in the winding streets, nearly too small for one car to pass, survey the flower boxes and window shutters, with a cat curled up in the sill, listen to the rhythm of the Seine River after a tour boat has passed (while licking a Bertillon ice cream cone, of course.) They want to feel the history and spirit of Paris sink into their skin as they live each magical moment there. They understand that there is more to Paris than the travel books tell you.

Along with being a top tourist destination, Paris is a residential city, home to just over 2 million people. Along the way, save some time to simply stroll the streets and absorb the culture, observe the daily habits of Parisians and the magic of Paris as a residential city. Savor the little-known corners of charm that the other tourist books don't talk about. Wander and see what else is waiting for you there.

The book in your hands will take into account both desires, the must-see destinations *and* the out-of-the way detours. First, each section will start with a list of top sights for that area. Then you will also find special suggestions of lesser-known treasures of this captivating city, all corners of it. There are a few walking tours, called Wanderings, scattered throughout. Lastly, I'll share my personal favorites from each section, from my years living there.

Once you've trekked around for a few days you'll see that Paris is a collection of villages and neighborhoods. It will lose any big-city intimidation and quickly become an old friend, as well as your second backyard. That's what it has been for me.

This book is different

With so many travel books written about the city of Paris, why another one? *This one is different* for a couple of reasons.

1.) Most travel books cover only the most popular and best-known sites of Paris within a few blocks from the city center (I call it Tourist Central.) However, there are many lesser-known discoveries elsewhere in the city. In this booklet you'll find BOTH, over 100 things to do and see **all across Paris**, in every district, including neighborhood wanderings (walking tours) and fun side trips. You'll discover the quirky, historic, or simply lovely, many of which you *won't* find in other travel books. You'll find Tourist Paris as well as Life Paris, where residents live and hang out. And I was a local there myself for many years, and I bring you an "insider flavor" in this guide.

There is beauty and fascination in every corner of this magical city. Why limit yourself to Tourist Central?

2.) Many travel books contain such an overwhelming flood of information (much of which you don't want or need) that it's a challenge to find what you're looking for, or even get a basic overview. These books will cost you between $20. and $30. and weigh a lot in your bag as you schlepp around the city. In contrast, *Magical Paris* is easy to use and easy to carry.

You won't be overwhelmed by *Magical Paris*. If you want the big picture neatly organized, you've got it. This book won't confuse or intimidate you. You can tuck it into a purse or bag or view it from your smart phone, tablet, or electronic reader. It costs less than lunch at a brasserie, for either the paper or electronic version. It's lightweight and has a helpful at-your-fingertips Index in the back.

Magical Paris is not a comprehensive guide to best restaurants, hotels, or flight deals. Other books and online resources will give you more of these if you desire. I will, however, include links to numerous web sites where you can do your own research before or during your trip. Then once you arrive in the enchanted city, *Magical Paris* will be almost indispensable for things to do and how to find them.

Go ahead, explore all the flavors Paris has to offer, from one end to the other, or in selective bites along the way.

How *Magical Paris* is organized

Most people agree that the best way see Paris is face to face and feet on the ground. That is why the information is arranged geographically, broken down into 5 sections starting in the center and going outwards clockwise. This will be helpful if you want to be methodical in your exploration or find things more easily.

This book is divided into 5 parts

Part One will provide basic information for getting around the city, as well as other helpful things to know. There's even a section on French pronunciation tips in case

you'd like to correctly say things on a menu or road sign (or be understood!)

Part Two will trek across the 5 sections of the city (Central, Northeast, Southeast, Southwest, and Northwest), taking you through each of the 20 arrondissments, or districts. Since 20 is a lot, I've grouped all these into 5 areas. A small map in each section will orient you. The dark line through the middle of the city indicates the River Seine, so you can easily find the right and left banks.

In each section you'll find: **First**, the most popular tourist sites and how to get there, **second**, worthwhile but lesser-known sights you may want to check out (called "Worth Seeing"). **Lastly**, I'll share a few of *my* personal favorites for that section.

A map in each section will show you where you are in relation to the whole city. For this edition of *Magical Paris* there isn't a Métro map, but here is a link that you can download onto your smart phone or tablet (including cool magnifying circle):

www.ratp.fr/en/plans-lignes

This link will appear at the beginning of the first section and just after the index, so you don't have to search the book for it. You can also get a free pocket Métro map (or a larger one) at the info booth at any Métro station.

Paris is not a hard city to navigate, especially if you keep referring to the district numbers to figure out where you are and where you want to be. Though not absolutely necessary, I recommend going to a kiosk (you'll see them frequently near Métro stops) and buying a small Paris map booklet, which costs around 8 € or so. This will give you detailed close-up maps of every numbered district in Paris, including all its streets. It also contains maps of the Métro, buses, trams, and suburban trains going out to the suburbs. That booklet can work hand-in-hand with *this* book to help you find your way, since I refer to the districts frequently. Having a map booklet also keeps you from having to open up a map 5 feet in any direction when you want to find something!

Part Three: The Near Paris section will list some close-at-hand treasures... towns, villages, and other excursions that are within an hour's travel from Paris. These are worth seeing if you have the time or want to get beyond the big city without spending more than a day. These towns are accessible by train as well as car.

Part Four: This section is called *Special Categories*, and contains a vast array of alphabetized information by category, depending on what you like or are looking for. Some examples of these are best parks, best cheap lunches, ideas for sports, family friendly, best hot chocolate, gluten-free, vegetarian, best brunches, etc.

Part Five: Last but not least, there is a comprehensive index so that you can find what you want to find in the booklet.

I hope you'll enjoy *Magical Paris.* I want to share it all with you because I don't want you to miss *anything* in my favorite city.

Map Links for Paris City and Public Transportation

The following link connects you to a map of Paris (streets) which you can zoom in or out if you have a tablet or smart phone. It's provided by the city of Paris. Go to the heading "Street Plans" and below, click on the link marked "Paris Map" in the following web site. http://en.parisinfo.com/how-to-get-to-and-around-paris/maps-and-plans

Free Métro maps are available at any Métro station information counter, in pocket or large print format. Just ask for a "plan du Métro, s'il vous plaît", (pronounced plon with a French nasal N.)

All over the city near Métro exits (either just before you exit the station or just outside) you will see posted maps of the neighborhood you're in. There are also maps of each neighborhood for purchase at vending machines and kiosks. Whatever hotel you are staying in will likely have free tourist maps, though these won't likely cover the entire city, just the central area.

The above link is the official website of the Paris convention and visitor's bureau, so it has other tips and ideas for visits, hotels, restaurants, walks, and more. There are also indications of where all the major tourist bureaus are throughout the city. It is a great resource to consult before and during your trip.

This link takes you to the downloadable map of the **transport systems** in Paris. www.ratp.fr/en/plans It includes Métro maps, bus and train maps, city and suburb maps, and schedule info at your fingertips on your smart phone or your tablet. It includes details on traffic including delays, how to find a specific stop, and other helpful things. It's mostly in French, but even without knowing French, you probably won't have any trouble using the Métro map itself.

There are various helpful maps here in English, including one for **wheelchair access**.

https://parisbytrain.com/map-paris-wheelchair-reduced-mobility-accessibility-metro-rer-bus-tram/

Book Stands along the Seine

Practical Information

If you're someone who likes to know what to expect in advance, this section is for you. You'll feel less nervous before arriving if you review a few of these details beforehand. If you're the more learn-as-you-discover type, just consult this section when you have a problem or a question. It's alphabetized for your convenience.

Airport Transport

<u>From the Charles de Gaulle Airport</u>

Roissy Bus This is a shuttle bus from the Charles de Gaulle Airport to the interior of Paris. https://bit.ly/2BBNH9p

The cost is 13€70 one way. It can be reserved online or purchased at any station or ticket machine in Paris. It takes 60-75 minutes and will take you to the center of Paris, letting you off at the Opera Garnier (11 rue Scribe), where you can connect to one of four Métro lines or the RER A train. Buses leave every 15-20 minutes going either way.

Air France Shuttle http://transfer.airport-paris.com/air-france-coach-service.htm This is available for all passengers, not just those on Air France. The service is called Le Bus Direct. Buy tickets at the Air

France ticket office or airport counter or online on Le Bus Direct website (read further.)

This shuttle operates at both Charles de Gaulle Roissy and Orly airports and takes passengers to 4 different locations around Paris. Four lines available, see below. For additional info, https://www.lebusdirect.com/en/

Orly South, gate L, arrivals. Orly West, gate D. Stops are: Montparnasse train station, Eiffel Tower, Trocadero, and Arc de Triomphe. Departs every 20 minutes. One way 12 € round trip, 20 €.

Charles de Gaulle (Roissy): Terminal 1: Gate 32. Terminal 2 EF: Gate E8/F9. Terminal 2 BD: Gate D14. Terminal 2AC: Gate C10. Goes to Eiffel Tower, Trocadero, Arc de Triomphe, and Porte Maillot. Leaves every 30 minutes and trip lasts 45-60 minutes on average. One way 17 €, round trip 30 €.

Charles de Gaulle to Orly All terminals. Departs every 20-30 minutes. Trip is 70 to 80 minutes, depending on traffic. One way 21 €, round trip 36 €.

Charles de Gaulle Roissy to Gare de Lyon and Gare Montparnasse All terminals. Departs every 30 minutes. Trip is 40 to 80 minutes, depending on traffic. One way, 17€. Round trip, 30 €.

RER B A regular train which goes from the Charles de Gaulle Airport to the center of Paris about every 10-15 minutes. Look for the sign "Paris by Train RER". You can get off the train at Gare du Nord or Châtelet or any other stop along the RER B and change to a Métro line, as well as on to some south suburbs. Cost: 10.30 € one way for ages 10 and over. Ages 4 to 10, 7 €. Under 7, free. Helpful info: parisbytrain.com/charles-de-gaulle-airport-cdg-to-paris-by-train/

Taxi You can take a taxi from either airport anywhere in Paris for between 40-50 €s. If you have lots of luggage or encounter traffic, it may cost a bit more. This is the easiest and most convenient way to go if you have a lot of things to carry and several people. Taxis are easy to find at either airport. I like the company G7 but there are several good ones. www.taxisg7.com/order-taxi/order-taxi-telephone

From the Orly Airport

Orlyval Shuttle
www.francetravelplanner.com/go/paris/trans/air/orlyval.html

This light rail shuttle will take you from/to Orly Airport to/from the town of Antony where you change to the RER B train (direction Mitry-Claye or Roissy) to continue to the center of Paris. The total trip takes about 35 minutes and departs every 4-7 minutes. Orly to Antony costs 9€30. Orly to central Paris is 12€05 each way.

Orlybus Catch this shuttle bus at gate H from Orly Sud. Orly Ouest, gate J. It costs 8€30 each way and will take you to the station Denfert Rochereau in Paris. There, you can then get the RER B to go elsewhere in Paris. Once you're in the city limits of Paris, the RER ticket is the same price as the regular Métro ticket, and you can use the same one until you leave the underground system.

https://www.ratp.fr/en/titres-et-tarifs/airport-tickets

Taxis from Orly will cost between 35-45 €.

American Embassy address 2 Avenue Gabriel, Paris 75008   Métro line 1, Concorde.
Phone: (33) 01 43 12 22 22.

ATM, credit, debit and cash Nowadays the cash question is much easier than it was in the days of traveler's checks. ATMs are the easiest and fastest way to get cash in France, and you can use either debit or credit cards.

In Paris it is easy to find banks if you know their names. Here are a few: Crédit Lyonnais, Société Générale, Crédit Agricole, HSBC, Banque Populaire, La BNP, and La Poste (yes, the post office too.) You must have your pin code to get cash out of one of these machines. Typically, there will be a daily limit, anywhere from 300 € to 800 €. I have never seen more than 800 €.

Fees vary, so you may want to check the difference between your credit and debit cards. Your home bank will likely charge you an international withdrawal fee, probably $3-5 per withdrawal for debit cards and possibly more for credit card cash advances. For purchases, some debit cards charge additional fees for each transaction as well. Many credit cards charge 3% on each international purchase, but credit cards that have no fee are available. Many banks in France are open on Saturdays but closed on Mondays. More and more you'll see bank branches that don't handle cash but have ATMs.

French stores take cards with the metallic chip but may still ask you to sign after your purchase, even if you know your pin. The necessity to sign your card is another reason to be very careful with it since anyone can sign your name if they get your card.

Bathrooms All over Paris you have clean, free kiosks (dome-shaped plastic, clearly marked) where you can answer nature's call. If you don't find one when you need it, you can always go into a café and ask to use the restroom (called *les toilettes*.) They aren't obligated to let you use it, if you haven't been a client there, but it might be worth a try. You can always try a bolder approach. Go in as if you are a client and look for a narrow stairway that either goes upstairs or downstairs (usually down.) This is the most frequent location, though some are on the same floor near the back. If anyone questions you say,

"Urgence" (emergency) and they may let you go. Don't forget to smile and say Merci.

Bicycles See also Vélib, the official Paris city bike rental. The following private bike companies also rent bikes and organize tours.

Freescoot. 63 quai de la Tournelle. Rental of bikes or scooters. Central Paris near Notre Dame. Online booking is available. Knowledgeable staff helps you pick the right bike or scooter. Tel. 33. (0)1.44.07.06.72 www.freescoot.fr/

Paris Vélos, C'est Sympa This company rents bikes and conducts tours. Located near Bastille at 22 rue Alphonse Baudin.

Boat Tours See *Special Categories* section at the end of this book (page 231) for companies and types of boat tours, from one-hour commented visits to dinner cruises.

Breakfast It is less common than in the past to have breakfast included in your hotel rate. Find out what's included. It may be worth the price. If your hotel charges over 10 € for beverages and bread only, you'll do better at a nearby café. If they have ham, eggs, bread, and hot drinks, (sometimes referred to as an English or American breakfast), it may be worth it. Sunday brunches have become very popular in Paris. The prices range from 10 € all the way up to 85! It depends on where you go (such as a fancy, famous hotel versus a corner bistro) and what they serve. Don't expect the same items as on a brunch menu you might be accustomed to. Remember, different can be great!

Business hours Stores typically open at 10 a.m. and close at 6, 7, or 8 p.m. Some grocery, like Monoprix, stores have longer hours and may be open until 10 p.m. In the suburbs and smaller stores in Paris, they may close for one to two hours during lunchtime. Banks still usually close for one to two hours at lunch, and those times vary, depending on the bank.

Buses See Local Transportation or Tour Buses

Canadian Embassy 35 Avenue Montaigne, 75008 Paris. Phone: (33) 01 44 43 29 00

Car Rental If you want to rent a car in Paris and go elsewhere outside the city, you should consider reserving it in advance. Rates can be lower in the U.S. than in

Europe, though some European companies, such as EuropCar, I have found to be very reasonable. www.europcar.com Also check SIXT-Eurorent. https://www.sixt.com/europe-car-rental/

You can pick up rental cars at airports and most train stations around the country. Sometimes you can get special deals through a flight/car rental package. Check these with travel companies online. See also *Driving and Parking*.

Crime and safety Paris is generally a safe city. The Métro is usually crowded until at least midnight, especially on weekends and in the summer. The RERs, however, are not as safe late at night, since they come and go into all the outer suburbs of Paris, some of which are less safe. While most areas are safe during the day, at night if you are alone, you should avoid areas like Gare du Nord and Gare de l'Est, and Barbés Rochechouart. If you're in a group or it's daytime, you should be fine in any of these places.

Wherever you are, be aware of pickpockets. Be careful when you get on and off the Métro or RER. It's the perfect opportunity for a pickpocket, since the doors will close, and he or she gets off with your stuff. Also, be careful about using a fancy phone in the Métro or RER, especially if you're sitting near the door. Beware of bands of young people. They aren't necessarily up to anything, but just be watchful. Some of these may be gangs who snatch nice cell phones or electronics on the train or stations. Don't forget to close your purse or backpack and don't leave wallets bulging accessibly out of your pockets. A small bag worn across the chest is very common for both men and women in France. You can keep your stuff in front and close to you, making it less available to pickpockets. In restaurants, beware of your bags and purses. Don't put a purse over the back of your chair, but rather keep it on your lap or between your feet under the table.

In our day there is also sometimes a concern about terror attacks. There is statistically little chance to be a victim of a terror attack. However, be watchful when in a large crowd. If you attend big events, such as fireworks, stay on the edges of the crowd and always be aware of what is going on around you. But don't forget to enjoy yourself too.

Currencies At the time of this writing the Euro equaled about 1.08 US dollars and .82 British pounds, 1.39 Canadian dollars, and 1.48 Australian dollars. For current rates check here: http://www.xe.com/

Customs Coming into France you will likely not be asked anything about what you are bringing in. As you leave the airport, just go toward the sign marked "Rien à declarer" or "Nothing to Declare". When you leave France, your suitcase might be searched at customs, but again, probably not. In all my years there, I might have had my bag searched once.

Discounts: Seniors, large family, students
For seniors, there are train discounts, but not as many
senior discounts as in the U.S. There are sometimes
senior discounts on museums, movie tickets, and
attractions. This is random and not necessarily frequent.
Be sure to look at signs or ask, all the same. Sometimes
large families can have discounts at certain places or on
trains. If you are getting tickets online and you have a
large family, look for the phrase "famille nombreuse".
Students have more discounts for museums, the Métro,
and inter-city train travel. Normally the cut-off is 26
years, though sometimes it is lower. Many museums
offer higher cut-offs for European residents.

Driving and parking Driving in Paris is a pain.
Avoid it if you can. It's not difficult to get around, but it
is congested, and parking is an even harder than driving.
If you insist on driving, be patient. Have a parking card
on you since parking meters don't take change anymore.
You can purchase these at a Tabac, the ubiquitous store
that also sells tobacco products, lottery tickets, phone
cards, and other tourist trinkets you might want (or not.)
Many places in Paris will have free parking on weekends
and the month of August, but this isn't likely in central
Paris. Finding an underground parking lot (look for the
blue sign with a large white "P" in the middle) is less
harrowing than parallel parking, but more expensive. As
for rentals to go somewhere else in France, it may be
cheaper to reserve it in the U.S. or your home country.

You may also benefit from some discounts that you wouldn't have in Europe. (See Car Rental.)

Driving in France can be expensive, due to the price of gas and the high cost of tolls. You can calculate the cost of a trip from one point to another on this website. http://www.lexilogos.com/itineraire_calcul.htm The site is in French. Temps means time, coût de trajet means cost of your trip. Driving may end up being reasonable if you have several people to share the costs, in comparison with plane or train travel. Getting out of Paris can require some patience, since the beltway, the *périphérique*, is crowded nearly all the time. It's the longest rush hour you've ever seen. Try to avoid early morning and late afternoon, and Sunday evenings as everyone returns from who-knows-where.

Here is a site in English that gives driving distances in kilometers (roughly half a mile) : http://distancecalculator.globefeed.com/france_distance_calculator.asp .

Autoroutes in France are well-maintained and fast. However, if you prefer a less-expensive scenic route, many of these routes also have corresponding Routes Nationales (shows up with a red N on your roadmap), which follow the same general routes, but are free. They are also longer, and this extra length varies. Check it out before you travel. If you want to see some countryside and speed of arrival isn't too important, you can try some of these roads. Be mindful that sometimes the first number doesn't correspond exactly (for example, you're looking for N60 from your map, you may see N360 on the road sign.) Usually only the first digit changes. Your road signs will not give you north, south etc. indicators, but will show you the name of a large city in that direction (not necessarily the next one you'll encounter.) For example, if you take the A6 highway to the south, you'll see the name Lyon and when you are leaving Paris, of course you're nowhere near Lyon, though you are traveling in the direction of Lyon. A word of caution: In the last few years, French highways have a zero-tolerance policy for speeding in an effort to reduce deaths on the roads. Don't speed at all unless you want to be liable for a fine (speed assessed by cameras.)

Duty Free Some shops in Paris advertise duty-free or tax-free. Typically, there is a lower limit of how much you have to spend before being eligible for this. Also, in duty-free shops at the airport, both Orly and Charles de Gaulle, you can do duty-free shopping. Present your receipts at customs to process your discount. For more info on this: https://en.parisinfo.com/shopping/visits-and-shopping-in-paris/duty-free-tax-free-shopping-in-paris

Electricity In France, electric current is 220. Many electronics these days convert automatically to European current but verify before you assume yours does. The easiest thing is to not bring items that don't convert. Computers usually do convert, but make sure. You can usually charge your cell phone on the USB port of your computer, rather than get an adaptor for it (though you will still need a plug adaptor for your computer or tablet.) This may be slower and might require you to be on your computer more than you want to be. An alternative would be to buy a French plug with a USB port, available at electronic or phone stores. Plugs in France have 2 rounded prongs instead of 2 flat ones. If you forget an adaptor, you can get one at BHV (a department store across Rue Rivoli from the Hotel de Ville) in the basement level.

Embassy Address See American Embassy or Canadian Embassy.

Getting around in Paris For a city layout, Métro layout, RER, tramway, buses, see the map links in the introduction. The Métro is easy to use. The direction is the endpoint, so see which direction you'd like to go and look at the endpoint, the name of the last station (called the terminus) and follow signs that correspond to that name. You'll need to switch lines from time to time, so just follow the appropriate signs, which are also color-coded. The same principle holds true for RER trains, which function just like Métro lines while in the city limits. RERs also continue out to the suburbs. Always keep your ticket on you until you exit the system and go outside. At times you'll need to pass your ticket a second time, such as when you change from a Métro to an RER or vice versa, and sometimes there will be a spot control, when you'll need to show your ticket to an agent or face a fine. You'll always need to pass your ticket to get out of RER stations. See local transportation for more on transport.

Hotels Below are some names of French chains, as well as travel sites that may guide you to the right hotels: First, check the official site for the Paris Convention and Visitors Bureau. http://en.parisinfo.com/   Here you'll find a wealth of tips and links for hotels, things to do, restaurants, shopping, and practical details. All sorts of lodging options are given, bed and breakfast, apartment/hotels, furnished rentals, camping, youth hostels, etc. Some good French chain hotels are Ibis, Campanile, Novotel, and Kyriad.

I recommend looking at the arrondissment (district) where you want to stay then search "hotels in Paris 12th", for example, giving the number you want and see what you find. Some local non-chain hotels are great and have French charm and good rates. Other suggestions follow:

For a familiar choice: There are 25 Holiday Inns around Paris. www.holidayinn.com

Tourist hotels by the City of Paris for youth, families, and individuals: reasonable and clean, usually on the outskirts of the city. Three locations in Paris, one outside the city. http://www.cisp.fr/   Check web site for pricing, addresses, reservations, and amenities.

<u>Youth Hostels</u> : Check for a broad range: www.hostels.com Below you'll find a few more.

1. Le D'Artagnan 80 Rue Vitruve, Porte de Bagnolet (33) 01 40 32 34 56. Listed as a youth hostel, but it's also for families, couples, individuals. Near the Porte de Bagnolet at the end of the line 3; other options are mentioned on the same site. http://www.hifrance.org/auberge-de-jeunesse/paris--le-d-artagnan/nuitees

2. Auberge Jules Ferry 8, Bd. Jules Ferry 75011 (Métro République, Goncourt) Tel: (33) 01 43 57 55 60

3. Auberge de Jeunesse Adveniat www.adveniat-paris.org (10, rue François 1er, in the 8th. E-mail adveniat@assomption.org Métro: Alma Marceau, Franklin D. Roosevelt)

4. BVJ (Bureau des Voyages de la Jeunesse) https://www.bvjhostelparis.com/en/ 20, rue Jean-Jacques Rousseau, in the 1st ; Phone : (33) 01 53 00 90 90. Email : bvj@wanadoo.fr 2 non-profit youth hostels in the center of Paris.

<u>Low-cost French chains</u>
Formule1
https://hotelf1.accor.com/map/index.en.shtml

Hotel Premiere Classe
http://www.premiereclasse.com/en

Apartment-Hotels

Citadines Apart-Hotel 16 locations around Paris

Air BnB: Don't forget this as an option for low-cost apartment rental. www.airbnb.com

Apartment rentals: www.VacationinParis.com or https://www.holidaylettings.co.uk/

Internet *(wifi zones; internet cafes, hotel internet)* Thanks to an effort by Paris' mayor, many places all over Paris, even parks and near public buildings, have wifi access. Of course, it isn't secure, and may be difficult to access, but it's there. Most hotels, cafés, and nearly all libraries have wifi access (though some hotels charge a fee for this), and there are also internet cafés you can find around the city. Some post offices also have internet stations you can use. If you do use internet at a restaurant or café, you'll have to vacate around mealtimes, unless you plan to eat there.

Local Transportation in Paris Métro and RER: The Metro/RER system is open from 5:30 am to 1:15 am. After that, there are night buses, the Noctilien line.

There are 2 types of trains in Paris, the subway system, or Métro, and the RER. The Métro cars are narrower, more numerous, and more frequent than RER trains.

They operate within the Paris city limits, though most lines extend one or two stops beyond to nearby suburbs.

The RER is a train. While inside the city limits, it functions just like a Métro, although a bit longer to change from one to the other. It requires passing your ticket a second time. There are 5 RER trains, each with several branches in either direction. They travel outside Paris to 6 zones of suburbs. The cost increases the further out you go. If you haven't purchased the proper fare (or if you've lost your ticket in transit), you will be unable to exit through the turnstile. Hang onto your ticket until you leave whichever system you are in. If you're caught without a ticket while in the system, you may have to pay a fine. Regular Métro tickets cover zones 1-2.

Endpoints of Métro lines or RERs will be clearly marked on all signs in the stations. Wherever two lines cross on your map, you can change lines there. To get out, the magic word is "Sortie". The phrase "Où est la sortie?" means "Where is the exit?" Useful, don't you think?

There are several types of tickets available for the Paris traveler. One of the best deals is the carnet (*car-nay*), or a book of 10 tickets. The average cost is only 1.69 per ticket (single tickets, 1.90 each), and if you plan to do a round trip a day plus a lot of walking, this may be all you need. You can buy it at the multi-language machines in Métro stations. This gives all the options and pricing for both single tickets or multi-day passes. https://www.ratp.fr/en/titres-et-tarifs It will enable you to choose the best options within Paris. The site also has helpful info on the Eurostar (to go to London), getting to Disneyland Paris, to Paris airports, and schedules for RER trains. See the introduction of this book for other sites where you can download a Métro or Paris map.

Multi-day passes The Paris Visit Pass offers a one or multi-day pass for transportation only. It offers unlimited travel for those days and some other discounts. (See other options below, including the best option, the Découverte.) *The Paris Pass is different* (see page 41) because it also includes attractions.

Current 2022 prices for multi-day Paris Visit Pass: (consecutive days, zones 1-3) 1, 2, 3, or 5 days. A pass for zones 1-5 is also available. This is only for transportation.

1 day Adults: 12€ Kids under 12: 6 €

2 days   Adults: 19€50   Kids under 12: 9€7

3 days   Adults 26€65   Kids under 12: 13€30

5 days Adults 38€35   Kids under 12: 19€15

A more reasonably-priced pass (with more benefits) is the Pass Navigo Découverte (also called the Navigo Weekly), which offers a Monday through Sunday pass for only 22€80 for zones 1 through 5. It covers the Métro, RER, trams, and buses. This is an excellent deal if you arrive on a Monday or Tuesday. If you arrive mid-week, this will be less of a benefit, and you'd be better off with a carnet or Paris Visit Pass. You can buy a Découverte up to midnight on Thursday for the same week or starting Friday for the following week. Purchase them online at www.Navigo.fr, at ticket counters, and at automatic machines in the station and even some ATM machines.

You'll have to find a ticket window that does sell tickets (an RER ticket window is your best bet), or at a Tourist Information Bureau. Monthly Navigo tickets are also available for 75€20 for all zones (less for fewer zones.)

Since the Découverte covers all 5 zones, you could use it for your transport into Paris on the RER (or back to the airport), provided you arrive at a time that the information counter is open, or you've bought it online in advance. You will have to buy a plastic holder (5 €, reusable for future visits) where you'll put your photo (selfies okay.) If you don't do this in advance, you can have a set of 4 passport photos made at booths found in many stations for about 6 €. You'll have to have the photo in place before you use the card for the first time. This link explains the week and month options, as well as the Decouverte and the Navigo transportation passes: https://parisbytrain.com/paris-train-metro-week-pass-navigo-decouverte/

Increasingly, ticket sales in Métro stations are being handled by automated machines. Information booth are still available but usually don't sell tickets. You can usually use your credit or debit card in these (and cash) without a problem.

Buses: Use Métro tickets or your multi-day pass on buses. You have to stamp Métro tickets a machine as you get on the bus (the machine is either at the front of the bus by the driver and/or in the middle, near the exit door.) You can use the same ticket for a change of buses, just like on the Métro. However, you cannot change from the Métro to the bus or vice versa with just one ticket. If you buy your ticket in a station, you can switch buses if you need a connection. If you buy your ticket on the bus from the driver, you can only use it for the one trip.

The advantage of buses is that you can see the city as you ride. It's quite pleasant (unless it's rush hour and you have an appointment.) Bus stops are easily identifiable on sidewalks and will travel in the direction of the side of the road you are on. Inside the bus there is a visual map of all the stops up near the ceiling on the sides, and there is sign overhead which lights up showing the upcoming stop. Pressing a button on the vertical poles notifies the driver that you'd like to get down at the next stop. Sometimes there will be a digital readout at the bus stop itself telling how long you'll have to wait for which bus. Bus routes are included on Métro maps.

Here are some nice routes which afford good views of Paris: Bus 69 (goes horizontally across town), 87 (left bank, 6th district, Eiffel Tower), 24 (east-west right bank, some locations on west bank), 63 (also east-west), 30, 48, 82.

Tramway There are 4 trams around the perimeter of Paris (and more outside Paris). Paris trams work with a Métro ticket as well. Tramlines are not connected to each other, but you can get down from one and onto another using the same ticket. Each one covers about one fourth of the city. They are quiet, clean, and pleasant. They have the sight-seeing advantages of buses without being subject to traffic slowdowns, since they have their own rail. The east Tram, or Tram 3b runs northeast from the Porte de Vincennes to Porte de la Chapelle. Tram 3a goes southeast from Porte de Vincenne to Pont du Garigliano.

To the west, Tram 2 starts at Porte de Versailles and runs up to La Défense (the corporate sky-scraper haven) and beyond to Pont de Bezons. All of the stops as well as beginning and end points are on the Métro maps which you can get for free in either large or small format at the information windows of Métro or RER stations.

Malls (and large supermarkets) Most malls are on the outer edges of Paris or in the suburbs, but a few can be found inside the city. On the outskirts there is Bercy 2, at the Porte de Bercy (not to be confused with the Bercy Métro station on the line 6), and at Porte de Bagnolet at the east end of the line 3. Inside Paris you'll find a large underground mall called Les Halles at Châtelet-Les Halles (recently renovated to a new level of chic), and at Place d'Italie, called Italie 2. At Italie 2 there is a Carrefour supermarket and at Porte de Bagnolet there is an Auchan supermarket. Both of these stores are much larger than the urban chains mentioned in the Supermarket section. (See Supermarkets)

Metric System A crash course: 1 kilometer is .6 miles, so you can roughly cut a mile in half to get a kilometer. Kilogram: Works the opposite way. A Kilo is 2.2 pounds, so just over double. Keep this in mind as you buy meat or produce. It may seem expensive, but it's over double the quantity if you are used to buying in pounds. Temperatures: There's no easy way to calculate in your head. Click here for some help: www.metric-conversions.org

Medical Care See Pharmacies and Medical

Museum Pass The Museum Pass is a ticket that give you access to a number of museums and monuments. The upgraded *Paris Pass* (page 41) includes a 2-day museum pass plus transportation and other attractions. Both passes enable you to jump ahead in line, which can be a huge advantage during the summer, when lines are longest at the most popular sites. They are available for 2, 4, and 6 days. Consult the site for current pricing, and to see if it's worth it to buy one. On the web site, you can buy tickets ahead and plan your visits by viewing what's included.

Current Museum Pass prices: 2 days for 52 €, 4 days for 66 €, 6 days for 78 €. This site will give you full information on the Museum Pass as well as other combination passes for sites and events.

Paris Pass pricing : see Paris Pass on the next page.
https://en.parisinfo.com/discovering-paris/info/guides/paris-museum-pass

Museum Tips Throughout most of the following sections, you'll find many museums. Most of these are closed one day per week, usually Monday or Tuesday. For safety, you are generally not allowed to bring luggage of any kind into the museum, though a few allow them in the coat check area. The websites will indicate if no luggage is permitted and if vaccines or masks are required. Some museums are free or a reduced price within one to two hours from closing time, so this is a bargain if you don't need a lot of time to visit. Many museums are free the first Sunday of each month. Some have various discounts, such as student, senior, unemployed, and large family. Some offer extended hours one night per week, usually Thursdays, which is sometimes called "Nocturne." Check the listing for the Museum Pass for museum passes for one or more days.

News in English Look for the International Herald Tribune at newsstands. It is in English. Also, you can sometimes get CNN on cable television around 7 am. Ask at your hotel for local schedules. And of course, your smart phone, computer, or tablet, has a huge variety of news in English.

Office of tourism This is the official site: http://en.parisinfo.com/   Here you'll find a lot of information to help you plan your days. Then the following site gives a list of the walk-in tourist offices, which are scattered around the city: http://en.parisinfo.com/practical-paris/our-welcome-centres

Paris Pass Not to be confused with the Paris Visit transportation pass, the Paris Pass includes both transportation and 75 attractions. Because it includes both, it costs more than both the Paris Visit and Museum Pass. It is an all-in-one visit and transport pass you can buy for 2, 3, 4, or 6 days. Adults: 2-day pass, 109 €, children 39 €. www.Parispass.com

Passports and visas Passports must be valid 6 months after your trip. There are no visa requirements for Americans or Canadians staying in France under 3 months. If your passport is lost or stolen, go to your embassy to ask for a replacement. (Address for American Embassy is listed above under American Embassy. Likewise, for the Canadian Embassy.)

Pharmacies and medical Pharmacies in Paris are abundant and easy to identify. Just look for a green neon plus sign. If it is a Sunday and the pharmacy near you is closed (as most will be), the door should post a phrase "Pharmacie de Garde", which gives an address of an open pharmacy. Pharmacists in France can give more health and medication information than those back home, so if you have certain symptoms, try to describe them to the local pharmacist and ask for a recommendation for an over-the-counter product. French medical care is very good, and less expensive than in the U.S. However, if you prefer, there is the American Hospital: 63 Boulevard Victor Hugo, Neuilly-sur-Seine. Phone number is (33) 01 46 41 25 25. The suburb of Neuilly-sur-Seine is accessible on the Métro line 1 going west toward La Défense.

Phone contact If you have a non-French phone, dial the "exit code" for your country (for the USA it is 011) then the French country code, 33, then the phone number, leaving off the 0. Most business phone numbers begin with 1. Some private phone numbers begin with other numbers such as 09, 06, or 07. In all of these cases, if you are calling from a non-French phone, after dialing the exit code for your country and the French country code, 33, dial the number without the zero. If you are using a phone that you purchased in France, omit the preceding numbers and dial beginning *with* the zero. A number beginning with 06 will be a cell phone number.

Every cell phone account has different roaming policies. Check your company's policy before going. Find out about the possibility of unlocking your phone before you leave. This will permit you to buy a French SIM card once you get there, which will allow you cheaper calling within France as well as calling home. Other options: phone applications such as What's App, Skype, and Viber can provide ways to text and call for free. You may be able to call for free from your hotel room using the hotel's wifi, depending on your device.

Phone booths hard to find. If you use one, you have to buy a phone card from a Tabac (a store that sells tobacco products as well as lottery tickets, phone, and parking cards, and sometimes souvenirs and trinkets.) Look for a red squared oval sign that says Tabac on it.

Post offices and mail French post offices are very efficient and well-equipped. In addition to normal postal functions, they have machines for many self-service transactions, a bank, and some even sell cell phones. The personnel are usually well-trained and helpful. Some may speak English, but don't expect it. Have your phrase book handy. Post card stamps will cost the same as for a regular letter, around 1€40. You can get international stamps at the machines, but normally they require a European bank card.

Supermarkets In Paris the common urban supermarket chains are Franprix, Monoprix, Simply, Leader Price, G20, or Aldi. Leader Price and Aldi are discount markets. The store Picard sells only frozen foods, but the range is anywhere from vegetables to complete gourmet meals and lavish desserts. Some stores do not provide grocery bags. At Monoprix for around 3 € you can get a very handy fabric bag (at the register) that folds up into itself and goes into a smaller bag that's easy to carry. This is a lifesaver if you need a small bag for just about anything (picnic, small grocery supplies, open market, spare comfy shoes (or band aids or socks...)

Taxis See Local Transportation or airport transportation.

Time Including 24 hour clock and daylight savings. For all scheduled events (trains, movies, plays, store hours, pretty much anything that has a fixed time) the French use the 24-hour clock. That means that anything between 1 and 12 is morning, and anything in the afternoon will start with 13 and go to 24, midnight. The way times are listed is with an h or H in between the hour and the minutes (this stands for "heure", which means hour in French.) For example, 1:30 in the afternoon will be listed as 13H30. Nine at night will be listed 21H00, and so on. Be familiar with these or carry a chart or index card around so you won't miss any trains or events.

In France daylight savings begins typically about 3 weeks later than in the U.S. Be sure to check online for the specific dates to know the difference on a given year, or in your particular country. This might be important if you have a phone date with a loved one back home during March or October when daylight savings begins or ends. During daylight savings, it stays light until after 10 pm.

Tipping and restaurants For meals and drinks, tips are included in the price that you pay, 15%. However, it is customary (though optional) to round your bill up to the nearest Euro or include between 20 centimes and a

Euro or two more if the service was good. Don't expect your waiter to be warm and tell you his or her name. It won't happen but doesn't mean they dislike you. It's just not part of the job nor the culture. They don't work for tips anyway. Some may seem abrupt, but it isn't personal. A typical scenario is a waiter/waitress arrives and asks if you are ready to order. They take your food order first, then your drink order, which is the opposite from the U.S. They have a lot of tables to look after, so don't expect lots of attention once you make your order. You might have to flag them down for something like more bread or another drink, and you'll most certainly have to flag them down for your bill. (Say, "L'addition, s'il vous plait" pronounced laddi-sionh, see voo play) and don't forget to smile. They don't expect this, but it doesn't hurt. Ever. And people really like it when you attempt their language, even if you butcher it (contrary to popular belief.) Trust me on this.

Tour Buses Several companies offer bus tours around Paris, with some allowing you to get on and off. Here are three: Tootbus Paris (formerly Open Tour, the green double-decker bus powered by electricity or natural gas.) The bus ride alone or bus/boat combination tickets are available. You can get them for 1, 2, or 3 days. There are 50 available stops plus several excursions. https://www.tootbus.com/en/paris/home . Check the website to see what other excursions are offered. Address: 13 rue Auber, 9th district.

Paris Tourism is a similar company that offers many combination tour packages around the city in a red double-decker bus. On and off touring is also available. http://www.francetourisme.fr/index_en.html

Paris City Vision This company also offers day trips and tours, including those to other areas near Paris, again with a double-decker bus. https://www.pariscityvision.com/

Trains (intercity/inter-country) Paris has 6 large train stations that service different cities and countries outside of Paris, and one small one, Gare de Bercy, which can take you south or east. These stations are usually also Métro stops. If you go to a train station by Métro, you'll exit the Métro system then look for the phrase "Grandes Lignes". This will point you to another area of the station where you will find the platforms for trains leaving the Paris city limits, whether suburbs, other cities in France, or other countries. As might be expected, the Gare du

Nord (north station) will take you to northern destinations, such as Lille, England, Brussels, etc. Gare de l'Est will take you toward the east. However, the Gare de Lyon takes you southward, toward the city of Lyon. Austerlitz, Montparnasse, and St. Lazare have still other destinations. The station will be marked on your ticket. You may need to go to that station to buy the ticket, unless you've purchased it in advance online. Having your e-ticket on you is a good thing, but you can also have it scanned by the conductor on your cell phone, if the scan code is visible. If you have a physical ticket, always date-stamp it in a small, strange-looking post at the doorway (usually yellow.) The verb is "composter" and has nothing to do with compost.

When booking tickets online, go to the SNCF web site and look for a ticket called Prems, which offers a discount. There are usually some restrictions, but if you get the Prems seats before they are sold out, you can get some excellent discounts. You can also get lower prices if you are flexible on the time and day you leave and come back. Check also *Ouigo*, a special group of routes within the TGV system. They go to specific locations, so but check your route to be sure. You can get some excellent pricing if you reserve well in advance. www.ouigo.com/

Here is a link directly to SNCF to look at train schedules: www.sncf-connect.com/

RailEurope is a sub-company of SNCF that markets to Americans and Canadians. They charge a booking fee. Go through SNCF directly to avoid this fee.

Eurail: If you are traveling around France and other countries of Europe, don't forget the Eurail pass. Check for different types of tickets: www.eurail.com/

Vélib Bicycles These are the gray bicycles you see all over the city. They are free for the first 30 minutes, but you'll pay for each partial half hour afterward. It might not end up being as reasonable as it is convenient, though some people love them. Electric bikes are now available. For more info: https://www.velib-metropole.fr/en_GB/discover/service See also *bicycles*.

Wheelchair Access Please see this link for more information on accessibility. https://wheelchairtravel.org/paris/ There are not elevators at every Métro station, but some do have them and quite a few RER stations do.

Pronunciation and Language

Here are some general guidelines for pronouncing French words.

When you see an "i" in the middle of a word or at the end, it is usually pronounced "ee". Example Rive Gauche (reeve go-sh).

When you see "au" it is pronounced "oh". Example: Tarte au chocolat (tarte oh shocolah.) Ch is pronounced sh.

Most of the time (not always) when you see words ending in a consonant, you don't pronounce that consonant. Exceptions are usually words ending in C, R, F, or L. Again, this also has exceptions. If a final consonant is followed by an e, you pronounce it.

When you see one "s" in the middle of a word, pronounce it like a Z. If it falls at the end of the word but is followed by a word beginning in a vowel, carry the Z sound over (don't make it silent.) Example: Nous allons   (we are going.... Nooz allon or Noo Zallon). If you see 2 sses, they are pronounced like an S.

When you see a vowel followed by an m or an n, it will be nasal. Examples, jambon... pronounce jam-bohn (ham), vin...vahn (wine), main...mahn (hand).

When you have a word starting with an i followed by an m or n, begin the word with an ahn or ahm nasal sound.

For example, do this with impossible (ahm-po-see-bluh) or interesant (ahn-terr-eh-sahn.)

Un: a for masculine nouns (un livre: a book) indefinite article, pronounced uhn.

Une: a for feminine nouns (une pomme: an apple) prounounced oon.

Le: the for masculine nouns (le livre: THE book) definite article, pronounced luh

La: the for feminine nouns (la banane: THE banana) pronounced lah

If you'd like to learn real French, instead of hacking through phrases, check my book *Real French for Travelers*. Through short, concise lessons, dialogues, and travel-related vocabulary lists, you'll be operational for your trips to France. It will also give you a good foundation if you decide to continue learning French.

BASIC GETTING AROUND

Vocabulary and pronunciation

La sortie : The exit   (la sortee)

L'entrée (f) : the entrance   (Lohn-tray)

L'accueil : welcome desk, information desk (lac-uh-ee)

La direction : the direction   (dee-rec-seeon)

Le panneau : the sign   (pann-oh)

Les grandes lignes : between-city trains   (grond leengs)

Un carnet: a book of 10 metro tickets   (car-nay)

Un billet: one ticket   (bee-yay)

Aller-simple : one-way trip   (allay-sampluh)

Aller-retour : round trip   (allay-retoor)

Un trajet : a trip   (trah-zhay)

Un tarif : the price for hotels, shows, travel (tar-eef)

Le prix: price for merchandise (pree)

La gare: the train station   (gahr)

Quel est le prix? What is the price? (Kell aye luh pree ?)

BASIC RESTAURANT VOCABULARY

L'addition, s'il vous plait: The check, please

La carte: the menu

Le Menu: fixed price menu, usually with 2-3 parts, appetizer, main dish, and dessert. Sometimes you must choose two out of three for the price listed. Not all restaurants offer this. On the other hand, some boulangeries (bakeries) offer this as a picnic, giving you the choice of a sandwich or piece of quiche, a canned drink, and a pastry. This is an economical way to have lunch.

Le plat du jour: special of the day. This is a main course that will usually only be served on that day, and isn't on the menu. There may also be an appetizer of the day or a dessert of the day. These specials will often be marked on a black chalk board outside the restaurant.

L'entrée: the appetizer, or first course. (Lon-tray)

Le plat: main course (le plah)

Le dessert (pronounce with an s sound, not a z sound)

For cooking meats: saignante or bleue (rare), à point (medium), and bien-cuite (well-done)

<u>Some hot drink vocabulary:</u>

(un) Thé: Tea, pronounced "tay".

Un crème: coffee with cream or milk already in it, like a café au lait.

Café alongé: Espresso diluted with water

Un noisette: an espresso with a tiny dollop of milk in it

<u>Fun drinks with light alcohol</u>

Kir: white wine with a flavored fruit syrup. The standard is currant syrup, called crème de cassis, but some establishments have other flavors. Kir royal: champagne with syrup.

(Un) Panaché: beer mixed with lemonade; it's quite palatable for the non-beer drinker!

(Un) Monaco: panache with flavored grenadine syrup.

BASIC COURTESY VOCABULARY

Merci, merci beaucoup: Thank you, thank you very much

Excusez-moi. Excusez-moi pour vous déranger: Excuse me. Excuse me for disturbing you

Allez-y : Go ahead (formal)   On y va: let's go (informal)

Pardon, excusez-moi : Pardon me, excuse me

De rien You're welcome (general), je vous en prie : You're welcome (formal) either works.

S'il vous plait: Please

BASIC MEDICAL VOCABULARY

Un hôpital: hospital, pronounced oh-pee-tahl

Une pharmacie: pharmacy, pronounced Fahr-mah-see

Malade: sick Je suis malade: I am sick (zhe swee malahd)

Je cherche un hôpital: I'm looking for a hospital (zhe shersh un oh-pee-tahl)

More French learning for travelers

Oliver's France offers a free mini-course (online videos) to learn French polite words and phrases and their correct pronunciation. See www.Oliversfrance.com, resource section in the top menu on the right.

For more in-depth language help, see the **Real French for Travelers Complete Online Course.** More information available on the Oliver's France website, as well as RealFrenchforTravelers.com. *Real French for Travelers,* the book, is described on the website and at the end of this book on page 265.

Owners of Magical Paris are entitled to a 20% discount on the full online course, Real French for Travelers with the code: LEARNFRENCH. Visit the site, realfrenchfortravelers.com. You'll be directed to the platform where you can use the code to purchase the online course.

Central Paris
Districts 1, 4, 5, 6

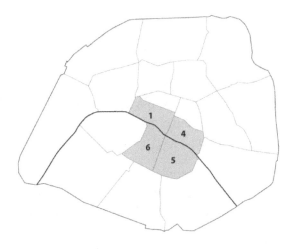

Your Métro map: https://www.ratp.fr/en/plans-lignes

Central

This is it, the heart and hub of Paris, a swath of land soaked in history and splendor, divided horizontally by the Seine River. Here you'll discover a dense cluster of many of the places you'll most want to see during your trip, in the first, fourth, fifth and sixth arrondissments, or districts. The sheer force of city energy will assail your senses in this central hub, which contains much of the bustle, most of the tourists, and most of the noise.

It's a great place to begin, especially if it's your first or second time in Paris. The first arrondissment in particular is a crossroad for the entire city. The largest station, Châtelet-Les Halles, which contains five Métro lines (1, 4, 7, 11, 14) and three suburban trains (RERs A, B, and D), is here in dead center. You'll likely change Métro lines frequently at Châtelet. The station is hectic, but well-marked. You might hear groups of classical or Eastern European musicians playing free concerts in the underground thoroughfare as you switch from one subway line to another.

The fourth district brims with attractive shopping streets, historic buildings, and much more you'll want to see (like the Pompidou Center, le Marais, and the Hotel de Ville.) It snuggles alongside the first district, sharing the northern Rive of the Seine. These two districts alone can supply more than a full day of wandering, visiting, and enjoying. You may want to set aside two or more days for this area, or even more if you are planning on visiting several museums. Another idea is to return there toward the end of your trip.

The fifth and sixth districts are located on the south bank (Rive Gauche) of the Seine. You can get there just by walking across one of the many bridges. In the 6th you'll find the Saint Germain des Près church and the neighborhood around it, including art galleries and the famed Garden of Luxembourg. Just to the east is the Latin Quarter in the 5th, with its student population, academic history, and quaint quirkiness.

Pick any district among the four to start, though you'll save time if you decide what you want to see before crossing a bridge to the opposite bank. But then, who wants to save time when you're on vacation in Paris? Just enjoy!

Main Sights in the 1st

Louvre and Tuileries Garden   Although Paris has over 150 museums, the Louvre is the best-known, as well as the largest and oldest. It has been a museum relatively recently, considering its long history.

The building was a fortress for Philippe August from the year 1190. It was completely rebuilt in 1546 on the orders of Francois I by architect Pierre Lescot. Influenced by Cardinal Richlieu, Louis XIII enlarged the building by four times. Many other royals lived there until 1871, when it was burned down during the Paris Commune uprising. It was restored in 1875.

It will take you the better part of a full day (or more, depending on your museum pace) to see everything inside. There are over 37,000 pieces to view.

<u>Hours</u>: Open 9am to 6pm every day except Tuesdays. Closed on Tuesdays.

<u>Admission</u>: 15 € at the museum, 17 € online (shorter lines.) Free under age 18, and age 26 for E.U. residents. http://www.louvre.fr/en   Included in the Museum Pass, and with faster entrance.

<u>Getting there</u>: Take the Métro line 1 to the station Palais Royal-Musée du Louvre. Then follow the crowds! Visit the web site before you go to see where to find different entrances, in case the main one is too crowded. The site is available in English.

Tuileries Adjoining the Louvre are the Tuileries Gardens. They are worth a stroll, and you'll find grassy areas where you can picnic or just lay in the sun, with the sound of the nearby fountain completely removing any tourist stress. Certain times of year you can see a Ferris wheel whirling gently on the horizon (or you can even ride on it.) More recently, however, the Ferris wheel can be found at Place de la Concorde, at the far end of the park.

On the grounds of the gardens lies the impressionist museum L'Orangerie (http://www.musee-orangerie.fr/), featuring Monet's water lilies, which cover several walls, and other notable works of art, special expositions, and sometimes concerts. Opn daily from 9 am to 6 pm. Closed Tuesdays.

Admission: 12€50 for adults, free under age 18. Free under age 26 for European residents. Next door is a modern art museum, Jeu de Paume.

<u>Getting there</u>: Métro line 1, Place de la Concorde.

The Ferris wheel near the Tuileries

Beaubourg Nearby is Beaubourg, a lively, mostly pedestrian area between the George Pompidou Center 4th and Les Halles (more on these in a moment...) You'll be surrounded by the animated energy flowing through a network of cobbled pedestrian streets that wind outward from the Renaissance *Fontaine des Innocents*. The fountain was erected in 1549, designed by Pierre Lescot, who was also the architect for the Louvre. The fountain was moved here to Beaubourg in the 18th century. It is the oldest fountain in Paris.

Here you'll find lots of crowds and festive ambiance, and of course, restaurants, shops, cafés, and street entertainment. There are chain and other fast-food restaurants as well as cafés and ethnic eateries. Underground is the recently renovated Forum des Halles mall. From the Châtelet station, follow signs to *Secteur Forum*. Other exits will lead you outside.

Getting there: Métro lines 1, 4, 7, 11, 14 or RER A, B, D to Châtelet.

Place Vendôme This famous square, or rather, octagon, in the 1st district features a tall obelisk in dead center, topped by a statue of Napoleon. Surrounding this is a large avenue with dozens of chic stores, formerly aristocratic mansions built in 1702. Now many of them are jewelry stores. Past residents of this square include Chopin and Coco Chanel. From there, stroll down Rue de Castiglione (where you can gaze on 45,000 Euro earrings or 30,000 Euro watches in stores like Cartier) toward the river. The opposite direction takes you to Rue de la Paix, which will lead you to the Opéra.

Worth Seeing in the 1st

Quais (riverbanks) along the Seine (1st and 4th) For a scenic riverside walk, find one of the descending stairways on either side of the Seine. Walk, sit, dream, or lunch on the centuries-old cobblestones along the gentle lapping of the Seine. You'll feel worlds away from the big city noise and traffic. You may wish to take a scenic cruise or dinner cruise on one of the boat tours. Some tours allow you to get on and off at various places around the city. Cruise personnel narrate the sites in several languages and give a good overview of the central part of the city. (Some boat companies: Batobus, Bateau-Mouche, Vedettes du Pont Neuf. See Boats in the Special Categories section, page 231.)

St-Eustache Church A beautiful Gothic structure, whose interior was inspired by Notre Dame. Begun in 1532, it took over 100 years to complete and also incorporates Renaissance features. Check out organ recitals on Sunday afternoons at 5:30. The writer Molière was buried here and Cardinal Richlieu was baptized here. Located near Les Halles and Rue Montorgeuil, at Place du Jour. Métro Chatelet-Les Halles, line 4.

The Galeries (or Passages) These are 19th century "malls", shopping centers tucked inside a building facade, topped by glass roofs. Most were built in the early 1800s and are still open today, filled with quaint and artsy shops. They are little-known sights of Old Paris and are found mostly in the 1st and 2nd districts. (See more in the 2nd district.)

Here are some of them: Go to Métro Line 1, Palais Royal-Musée du Louvre stop. Go out towards Rue de Valois (runs alongside the Jardin du Palais Royal.) Turn right at

Rue Montesquieu and at you'll see *Passage Verité*. After your visit there, go to the end of Montesquieu and you'll see *Galérie Vero-Dodat*, opened in 1826. It was the first Galérie to have gas lighting. http://bit.ly/1LKrXCh

Passages can be found in the 1st, 2nd, 9th, and 10th districts. See more in the 2nd (Northeast) district.

A 19th century Galerie

Rue Montorgeuil A vibrant, mostly pedestrian street lined with shops and restaurants, as well as a juice shop, pharmacies, gourmet candy and flower shops, and ice cream. It's a haven for foodies and ambiance-seekers. There is a permanent open market, and many quality foods (some say among the best in Paris) are available in small shops— butchers, cheese shops, bakeries—just like in the old days. You'll find ethnic restaurants as well as historic favorites like L'Escargot, at # 38, founded in 1875. Impressionist Claude Monet captured this road in his painting *Rue Montorgueil*, with festive flags filling the street with color. Camille Pissaro, another renowned impressionist, also painted this bustling street.

<u>Getting there</u>: Métro Line 4, Les Halles.

French pastry is as good as it looks!

Chatêlet Les Halles In 1135, Les Halles was a wholesale open market, selling meats, fruits, and vegetables, and many other things. Because of population growth in the 16th century, only food merchants were allowed to sell their goods here. In the 1800s, wide avenues were created all around the area.

Then in 1969, the market was moved to the outskirts of Paris and the area was repurposed for shopping, as it is today. Though shops and restaurants exist all around in the Beaubourg labyrinth, there is also a huge underground mall, opened in 1979. It has recently undergone a massive renovation, finished in 2016.

After you've strolled around Beaubourg, you can access the mall by escalator at Les Halles to see the newly upscale shopping cavern that covers several floors. If you get off at Châtelet and want to go directly to the mall, follow signs to the Secteur Forum des Halles. There you'll find shops galore (normal mall fare, not luxury shopping), as well as two UGC cinemas.

Getting there: Métro 4, Les Halles, or RER Châtelet-Les Halles. Access is explained in the above paragraph. Access to Les Halles is easier if you take the Métro and follow signs to the Forum des Halles. From outside, follow signs and look for a large entrance with an escalator going down.

Au Pied de Cochon, 6 rue Coquillière. This short little street (not that short since it continues on from Rambuteau then changes names) lies just outside of the far end of Les Halles, the closest exit to the bigger UGC movie theatre. The restaurant Au Pied de Cochon (pig's foot) celebrates one of Paris' old delicacies in an historic restaurant, open since 1946, and is open all night. I haven't had the courage to try a pig's foot, but my friend

Françoise says they're delicious. Of course, they also serve other dishes, such as seafood. The street is lined with shady trees and more cute restaurants. It isn't far from Rue Montorgeuil toward your right (just after the imposing Saint Eustache church), nor from Rue du Louvre to the left. If you turn left at the end of this short road, it will take you back toward the Seine and towards the Louvre Museum.

Rue de Rivoli The attraction here is shopping: moderately-priced clothing and shoe stores line both sides of this incredibly busy street along Rivoli near the Châtelet area. In fact, Rivoli has lots of shopping as far as you go towards the east, until the road ends in the Marais neighborhood. If you're into more chic shopping, head up the same road in the other direction, towards the Louvre. Go to the arches facing the Tuileries. There are many typical Paris souvenir shops, but you'll also find luxury as well as duty-free shopping. Find more luxury shopping on Rue Faubourg St-Honoré or the Champs-Elysées (both in the 8th) and many other places especially in the 1st, 7th, 8th, and 9th. (See also pages 244-245.)

Getting there: Take Métro line 1 to Châtelet, Rivoli exit.

Place Dauphine Believe it or not, there is a relatively quiet hidden place on the busy island of Ile de la Cité, near the courthouse. Go to the western tip of the larger island and you'll see a small road (Rue Henri Robert) leading into a shady courtyard, surrounded on either side by quiet hotels and small restaurants. There may be a game of boules going on in the center. This serene square was created by Henry IV in 1607 in honor of his son, called the Dauphin, or future ruler. The Pont Neuf, a bridge that connects the right and left banks, crosses over the point of the island where the Place Dauphine is.

Paris Plage (1st & 4th, North Bank): Every year from mid-July to mid-August the beach comes to Paris, specifically, the north bank of the Ile de la Cité. The road is closed (now permanently reserved for pedestrians) and tons of sand as well as potted palms and lawn chairs are brought in to create a beach in the center of Paris. Enjoy strolling, dancing, misting yourself in the mist garden on a hot day, playing games and eating ice cream and crêpes. For the last several years Paris Plage has also taken place at the Bassin de la Villette, an animated canal area near Métro Stalingrad (19th). It's less hectic and crowded than the original location, and quite pleasant.

Palais Royal A palace once called the Palais-Cardinal, is adjoined by a small park with a lovely fountain and what looks like an oversized checkerboard, a sculpture by Daniel Buren. The Palace was the residence of Cardinal Richlieu, who became prime minister in 1624. Today the building is used by various government ministries, but you are free to wander about the lovely gardens.

<u>Getting there</u>: Take Métro line 1 to Palais Royal-Musée du Louvre and go north across Rue Rivoli and Rue St. Honoré.

Musée des Arts Décoratifs Part of a group of museums. See details on page 197, Nissim Comondo.

My Favorites in the 1st

Beaubourg (1st) It's noisy and crowded, very touristy, but fun.

Les Péniches (1st): A péniche is a small barge parked in the Seine and transformed into a pub or restaurant. A cluster of these stationary bar/restaurants are moored across the river from the Notre Dame Cathedral. Several more line the banks of the 13th, southeast. Some are lively dance spots (see After Work, Le Quai 21 Quai Anatole France in the 7th.) It's fun, if you think you'd like a floating nightclub. Though some are stationary, a few companies offer a "croisière", or a cruise or dinner cruise.

A péniche floats in the Seine

Tarte Tatin *Chez Panis*: Tarte Tatin is a French specialty apple pie, with thick chunks of apple cooked until very soft and melt-in-your-mouth good. Go from the Notre Dame Cathedral to its nearest bridge and cross. Look for this brasserie, Café Panis, on the left bank close to the river. Get it with ice cream or crème fraîche (my preference.) This dessert is a classic available throughout France.

Paris 4th

To visit the 4th district, you may want to start on the east end of the Ile de la Cité, the larger of the two islands in the Seine. This part of Paris is *medieval* Paris, gothic Paris. This is the city's birthplace (some say 10,000 years ago!) Centuries of French kings ruled here until the 14th century, when they started moving out to the "Burbs", such as Versailles and later to the Loire Valley. On Ile de la Cité you'll find the most famous historic prison, La Conciergerie, where Marie Antoinette was an inmate. Nearby is the ancient hospital, L'Hôtel Dieu, where at one time the dead were tossed onto boats in the Seine. It was used as a hospital up to recently.

If you observe the island, you'll see that it still looks medieval and gothic, though comfortably nestled in a modern city. On this island resides the Sainte Chapelle, Notre Dame, and a flower market near the Métro stop Cité. Square du Vert Galant is a park which honors Henri IV, whose statue guards the entrance. It sits on the northwestern pointy end of the island with a view of Pont Neuf. (This corner of the island sits just over the border in the 1st, if you're trying to find it on your numbered map.)

A word on Bridges.... The statistics vary, but there are at least 28 bridges in Paris (not including traffic bridges towards the periphérique, Métro trestles, or pedestrian passages and bridges). Regardless of the number, they are unquestionably romantic and scenic. You can get some breathtaking photos at different times of day, including distant shots of the Eiffel Tower or the Hotel de Ville lit up at night. The oldest of them is, ironically, called the Pont Neuf, or New Bridge, begun in 1578 and completed in 1604.

Susan suggests seeing

Main Sights in the 4th

Sainte Chapelle on the Ile de la Cité, is a small but lovely example of Gothic architecture. It was completed in 1248, commissioned by King Louis IX to house the holy relic of the Crown of Thorns, and other Passion relics. The 15 panels of stained glass that grace the walls, stunning in sunlight, comprise the largest collection of 13th century stained glass in the world. Over half is original.

<u>Hours</u>: Usual hours: Open April 1-September 30 from 9:00 to 7 pm, Monday through Sunday. From October 1 to March 31, open 9 am – 5 pm.

La Sainte Chapelle

<u>Admission</u>: Adults: 11€50; under 18 free, E.U. residents under 26 free. Combination ticket with the Conciergerie: 18€50, only available online. Covered by Museum Pass. Not free the first Sunday. http://www.sainte-chapelle.fr/en/

<u>Getting there:</u> Métro Line 4, stop at Cité. Go across the Boulevard du Palais.

Conciergerie   This was the first royal palace in the oldest part of medieval Paris. During the French Revolution it was used as a prison. Over two thousand prisoners, including Marie Antoinette, were held there prior to their execution. Today you can see both the palace and the prison. It's eerie to think that this building is actually part of the complex including present day justice buildings.

http://www.paris-conciergerie.fr/en

<u>Hours</u>: Usual hours: Open daily 9:30 – 6 pm.

<u>Admission</u>: 11€50 for adults; free under 18. Free under 26 residents of E. U. Combination tickets with the Sainte Chapelle are available, 18€50 (see Saint Chapelle.) Included in the Museum Pass.

<u>Getting there</u>: Métro: line 1, Cité. The building sits on the north bank of the Ile de la Cité (the bigger island).

71

Pompidou Center   This center, well-known for the funky architecture whose innards are on the outside, houses the largest modern art museum in Europe. Opened in 1977, it also contains a substantial public library and a café with a view of Paris on the top floor, shows and concerts, and the Galerie des Enfants, especially for children. Outside the center is a fun neighborhood flowing into the Beaubourg area. Here there's plenty to see and experience in every direction. Nearby you'll see the Stravinsky Fountain (named in Stravinsky's honor), a whimsical collection of 16 moving toy-like sculptures in a shallow, square fountain surrounded by crêperies, restaurants, and teashops. www.centrepompidou.fr/en/

Hours: The Pompidou Center is open Wednesday through Monday, 11 am to 10 pm. Closed Tuesdays. Library is open from 12 noon to 10 pm. Tours in English are given Saturdays at 12 noon.

Admission: Adults, 14 €. Ages 18-25, 11 €. Under 18, free. Other prices for terrace view (5 €.) Terrace is free for E.U. members under 26, but a ticket is required. Free the first Sunday of the month. Guided tours in French, 4€50, films (6 €). Show and concert, 10-18 €, depending on show. General Info: (33) 01 44 78 12 33. Included in Museum Pass.

Getting there: Métro Line 11, Rambuteau

Notre Dame Cathedral (*Note*: Following a fire in 2019, the Cathedral is closed until 2024. The exterior, however, is well worth a visit and photo.) This is arguably one of the best-known cathedrals in the world, in the beautiful French Gothic style. An architectural wonder, one of the first to use flying buttresses, it was begun in 1163 and completed in 1345. Climb to the top, if you can deal with 387 steps. The view will be worth it. It's as beautiful (or more so) on the outside than the inside. Don't forget to circle all the way around the outside of the church to see all the aspects of its stunning architecture. Going into the church is free. Climbing the stairs and visiting the crypt require a small charge. If you have time, try to take in an evening candlelit Mass, or catch a free organ concert. Sometimes concerts will be posted outside or online.

Getting there: take Métro line 4 to Cite or RER B to St. Michel/Notre Dame.

Hotel de Ville, or city hall. This has been the location of the municipality of Paris since 1357. Today it houses local administration and the mayor's office and hosts receptions for foreign and local dignitaries. The current gorgeous building was completed in 1892, following several uprisings, a fire, and several hundred years of turbulent history starting in 1533. Visits are free and there is always a free exhibition of art or photography on the premises.

Getting there: Take Métro Line 1 to Hotel de Ville

Le Marais This was once an upper-class neighborhood, or *quartier*, and is one of the oldest in Paris, featuring the Place des Vosges. During the Revolution mayhem reigned (see below) and everything fell into disrepair. Later it was refurbished and regained its privilege of housing the upper classes. Nowadays in this neighborhood you'll find trendy, expensive shops, cute streets, restaurants, and architecture, a higher-than-average gay population, and the Jewish district. Rue de Rosiers is the headquarters for the coveted felafel sandwiches (where long lines of people wait to get them), as well as several Jewish bakeries and jewelry/gift stores. Nearby is the Memorial of the Shoah, or French Jewish deportation during World War II. This museum is free, a troubling and moving tribute to French Jewish adults and children who lost their lives. Address: 17 rue Geoffroy l'Asnier. www.memorialdelashoah.org

Getting there: One way to get to the Marais is by way of the Bastille area. Take Métro line 1, 5, or 8 to the Bastille stop. Walk west across Rue Beaumarchais, turn right and go up the road a few streets, then turn left on Rue du Pas de la Mule. This route will lead you past the Place des Vosges (see following) and into the heart of the Marais.

A more direct access is to take Métro line 1 to St. Paul, cross Rue Rivoli and enter the neighborhood by way of Rue Pavée. To reach the Place des Vosges, continue straight to Rue Francs Bourgeois and turn right. You can then continue to Place de la Bastille if you want by doing the above steps in reverse.

The Place des Vosges represents medieval Paris as it was up to the mid-1800s. The Place was built in 1605 by Henry IV as the neighborhood for French aristocracy. These elegant homes line up in a square surrounding a small park. Later the Revolution chased the residents out and it went through its slum period. Today it is once again a chic, expensive, and desirable place to live. Victor Hugo lived at # 6, which is now a small, free museum highlighting his life and work.

<u>Getting there</u>: see above

Ile Saint Louis

Worth Seeing in the 4th

Quais (riverbanks) along the Seine (1st and 4th). Find stairways going down to the riverfront and enjoy the stroll.

Ile Saint Louis This smaller of the two islands in the Seine has a quiet charm all its own (although lately it seems the tourists have discovered it in hoards.) Here you'll find flower shops, art galleries, many restaurants, and famous Bertillon ice cream. Then go down to the riverfront below to enjoy the quiet waters as you lick your ice cream. Many notable residents, including Marie Curie, have lived on this island. Currently, it's expensive to live here. Always free, though, for a good stroll.

St-Louis-en-l'Ile A church with a Jesuit baroque interior; built between 1664 and 1726. You'll find it at 19 bis rue St. Louis en L'Ile, on the Ile de Saint Louis, the smaller of the two islands.

Musée Carnavalet on Rue des Francs Bourgeois. This small, free museum sits technically in the 3rd district, but it's easier to see it as you're wandering through the 4th in the Place des Vosges area. The museum features the history of Paris. The website is in French, but you can access the English translation by clicking on ENG in the upper right corner.
http://www.carnavalet.paris.fr/fr/musee-carnavalet

Open 10-6 daily. Closed Monday. An admission fee will apply for conferences, special temporary exhibits, and cultural activities.

St-Merri Church This medieval church site is from the 7th century, the burial place for St. Méderic, abbot of St. Martin d'Autun. The current Gothic building was built in the early 1500s. The inside is worth a look. The church contains the oldest bell in Paris, from 1331 and stained glass from the 16th century. Access by rue Saint Martin or 76 rue de la Verrerie.

The Pavillon-Arsenal is a fascinating, free museum for those interested in urban history and current building projects in Paris. The building alone is worth going to see. It's best said in their official description: "The Pavillon-Arsenal is the center for information, documentation, and exhibits for urban planning and architecture of Paris and the Parisian metropolis."
There you'll see large maps of the city, historical artifacts, and discussions on current architecture projects. http://www.pavillon-arsenal.com/en/

Getting there: 21 Boulevard Moreland, 4th.

Places des Vosges, Le Marais

My Favorites in the 4th

Ile Saint Louis On the north side of the island is a lovely tree-lined avenue, with benches calmly overlooking the Seine towards the north bank. You can perch on one of these benches for a picnic, or head down the eastern staircase to river level for shady tranquility.

Riverbanks Sit still and listen to the water lapping the ancient stones; picnic along the Seine with the noisy streets far and away above you. The southern bank of the island is sunnier.

Pedestrian streets around Pompidou Center This is a fun area to stroll and absorb the city energy. Cobbled streets surround the Pompidou Center, and the large open pavement in front of the museum attracts musicians, tired tourists, and picnickers.

Neighborhood Wanderings The following streets are recommended for the Marais wandering tour: Sainte Croix de la Bretonne, Rue de Rosiers; Place des Vosges, Rue des Francs Bourgeois.

Paris 5th

The Fifth district is best known for the Latin Quarter and the thousands of students who have rambled through its narrow streets for seven centuries. The Sorbonne is the most renowned and oldest of the many campuses of the University of Paris as well as other institutions scattered through the 5th and 6th districts. Back in the 13th century, when the Sorbonne was founded, Latin was the international language of higher learning, hence the name Latin Quarter.

Today this area is energized by students and tourists alike, and there is plenty to see aside from educational buildings. The style of the architecture and city layout is unique to the Latin Quarter. You won't want to miss the notable landmarks. Scattered through this area are many new and used bookstores, as you might expect, with so many students. At the end of this section is a 5th District Wandering you may enjoy. There is a lot to see in the 5th!

Main Sights in the 5th

The Latin Quarter This area extends across the 5th district. One of its best-known enclaves is nestled in cobbled pedestrian streets nearby the Place Saint Michel. The winding streets, Rue de La Harpe, Rue Saint Séverin, and Rue de la Huchette, are mazelike paths filled with pedestrian bustle, plenty of restaurants, snack and souvenir shops, and loads of tourists. It's energetic, quaint, and so Paris.

Getting there: You can get here on the RER B Saint Michel/Notre Dame or Métro line 4 Saint Michel. You can also get there on the line 10 to Cluny, where there is also the Cluny Museum.

Place Saint Michel The monument that gives St. Michel its name is a fountain with a large statue of the archangel Michael. The monument was completed in 1860, and quite a number of artists were involved in its creation. The statue is decked on either side by water-spouting winged dragons. As for the human element, you'll see throngs of people there to meet someone or watch the street entertainment, or just passing to the other side. It sits on the dividing line between the 5th and 6th districts.

Getting there: Take the Métro (line 4) to St. Michel or RER B station St. Michel/Notre Dame.

The Panthéon was originally a church dedicated to Saint Genevieve, the patron saint of Paris. After the Revolution, it became a mausoleum where famous citizens were buried, among them Victor Hugo, Voltaire, Jean-Jacques Rousseau, Alexandre Dumas (author of The Three Musketeers), Pierre and Marie Curie, and French resistance fighter, Jean Moulin. This expansive building is a Neoclassical monument modeled after the Roman Pantheon, with impressive architecture inside and out.

Hours: Open 10am to 6:30 pm in summer (April 1-September 30). Closes at 6 in winter.

Admission: 11€50. Under 18, free. Free under age 26 for residents of the European Union. Included in Museum Pass.

Getting there: Take Métro line 10 Cardinal Lemoine or RER B Luxembourg and go up Rue Sufflot. http://pantheon.monuments-nationaux.fr/ Covered by the Paris Museum Pass.

Les Salons du Panthéon While you're in the neighborhood, stop in for some refreshment at a unique tearoom designed by Catherine Deneuve herself. It is also occasionally frequented by actors, producers, and directors. On the terrace outside or snuggled in a comfy couch inside, you can enjoy lunch or tea until 6 pm. A light lunch is available from 12:30 to 3, then the tearoom is open until 6. Prices for meals range from 16 to 32 €. Wine and desserts (some gluten-free) also available. Closed Saturday and Sunday.

Getting there: Rue 13 Victor Cousin, a couple of blocks from the Jardin de Luxembourg, and right near the Sorbonne. Métro 10 Cluny-La Sorbonne or RER B Luxembourg.

Rue Mouffetard and Place Contrescarp. The Rue extends several blocks on one of the oldest streets in Paris, lined now with restaurants and shops. Lots of ambiance here and on surrounding streets, Rue Lacepède, Rue Descartes and Rue Thouin. Right in the middle sits the Place Contrescarp, a circle surrounded by more cute eateries and, sometimes, street entertainment. On Rue Mouffetard you'll find: Mexican, Lebanese, Japanese, Spanish, American, French, Greek, and Vegan food (did I miss any?) If you don't satisfy your appetite on Rue Mouffetard, just keep going until you cross paths with Rue Pot de Fer, a narrow, medieval-looking pedestrian street lined on either side with more restaurants. This area is lively and crowded in the afternoon and evening, but a bit dead in the morning. The exception to that is the open market at Place Monge, parallel to the Rue Mouffetard.

Getting there: Take the Métro line 7 and get off at Place Monge. Go towards Rue Ortolan (going away from the bigger street, Rue Monge) and this will lead you to Rue Mouffetard, roughly parallel to Rue Monge.

Cluny Museum, Musée de Cluny, also known as the Musée National du Moyen Age (National Museum of the Middle Ages.) The best-known artifact is a series of six Tapestries which, together, are called La Dame a la Licorne (The Lady and the Unicorn.) The tapestries date from the 15th century. The museum was built on the ruins of 3rd-century Gallo-Roman baths (Thermes de Cluny.) The first structure on top of the bath was the town house of the Abbots of Cluny in 1334, then rebuilt between 1485 and 1510 in Gothic and Renaissance styles. As you approach from the Boulevard Saint Michel, the museum has what might appear to have a worksite in the front, partitioned off by a wire fence. But look closer. It's actually a centuries-old Roman bath! Of course, you'll get a better look from inside. Note: at the time of this writing there is long-term renovation work being done on the outside. However, the museum is still open, and you'll be directed to an alternate entrance. Suitcases, backpacks, and large bags are not allowed, for security reasons.

Hours: Open 9:15 am to 5:45 pm every day except Tuesday.

Admission: 5€. Free for those under age 18; E.U. residents, free under age 26. Free the first Sunday of the month. Covered by the Museum Pass.

Getting there: Take Métro line 10 to Cluny/Sorbonne or the Line 4, St. Michel and walk south on Blvd. St. Michel. http://www.musee-moyenage.fr/

Worth Seeing in 5th

La Sorbonne Founded in 1237, the University of Paris is one of the oldest in Europe. The Sorbonne building housed one of the earliest colleges of the university. Currently, the Sorbonne still holds classes at this location and houses the administrative office of the 13 campuses of the University of Paris.

Getting there: From the Saint Michel Métro, continue south on Boulevard Saint Michel. After you pass the Rue des Écoles you'll see the building on your left (Place de la Sorbonne) behind the cafés and fountain.

Eglise St. Etienne du Mont (right next to the Panthéon.) This is one of the most beautiful churches I have seen in Paris, inside and out. The interior is light in both color and atmosphere, lovely and airy, with sculpted balconies extending across the middle and on either side of the vaulted space. Next to the Panthéon.

La Mosquée (Mosque) de Paris From Rue Mouffetard, cross over the Rue de l'Epée de Bois, then cross over Place Monge and Rue Monge. These will be the opposite direction from Rue Mouffetard. Go down Place du Puits de l'Ermite and you'll run into one of Paris' largest Mosques. You can go inside for a 30-minute tour (3 €) where you can observe the ornate Arabic mosaic, sculpted plaster and carved cedar wood (direct from Lebanon, no less.) You can't enter the prayer room but sometimes can look inside from the doorway. After you exit, go clear around to the other side for the café, a restaurant, and a hamam (Turkish bath), with massages and other treatments.

I have eaten in the restaurant once and had an unforgettable lamb tajine. There are several varieties of tajine as well as cous cous. The outside café on a tree-shaded terrace just in front of the building is also a special treat.

Getting there: Take Métro line 7 to Rue Monge. Follow indications in the beginning of this paragraph.

Les Arènes de Lutèce This may not seem much to look at, but it is THE oldest monument of any kind anywhere in Paris. Here you will see the remains of a first century Roman arena, where gladiator fights and wild animal shows were held. Though much has been destroyed and some rebuilt over the centuries, you can still see some original arches, stonework, and animal holding areas.

Getting there: Take Métro line 7 to Monge (to the south) or Cardinal Lemoine (to the north) The Arènes are between these, accessible from Rue des Arènes, between Rue Rollin and Rue Linné.

The following areas are close together in the eastern part of the 5th, near the riverbank. You could easily walk from one to another if you want.

Institut du Monde Arabe (Arab World Institute) Continuing on the Arabic theme, in the same district you'll see the Arab World Institute. Here you'll find art expositions, educational programs, music, a library, and a beautiful view from the terrace-restaurant (Lebanese) on the top floor. You can also just look out from the terrace without dining. The building is an architectural wonder, covered with panels that work like hundreds of camera lenses, letting in measured amounts of sunlight. It's worth a look even just for the outside of the building, though there's much more inside as well. Website in French: www.imarabe.org/en/

Here's a site in English with photos for all of you fans of architecture: http://www.archdaily.com/162101/ad-classics-institut-du-monde-arabe-jean-nouvel/

The Institut is open Tuesday, Wednesday, Friday from 10 to 6. Otherwise, 10 am to 7 pm. Closed on Mondays, but during the year it might be closed at other times for religious holidays.

<u>Admission</u>: 8 €; 4 € for non-E.U. residents under age 26, and free for E.U. residents under age 26. Group rates available (6 people minimum). Tickets available online.

<u>Getting there</u>: Take Métro line 7 to Cardinal Lemoine. Go east on Rue du Cardinal Lemoine, and cross the street towards Rue des Fosses St. Bernard. The address of the institute is 5 rue des Fosse Saint Bernard.

Jardin des Plantes After leaving the mosque, you're not far from the Jardin des Plantes. The original name of this garden was The Royal Garden of Medicinal Plants and was established in 1635. Walk south along the Quai Saint Bernard, which runs along the Seine. This is one of the two largest botanical gardens of Paris, with 11 individual gardens inside. The other one, Le Parc Floral, is just outside the city limits. (See 12th arrondissment for the Parc Floral.) At the Jardin des Plantes there are also 3 natural history museums, all housed in 19th century buildings:

La Grande Galerie de l'Evolution (Great Hall of Evolution), which has an impressive display of 7000 species on 4 floors, including the skeleton of a blue whale and a stuffed rhinoceros that once was a pet of Louis XV. www.grandegaleriedelevolution.fr

<u>Hours</u>: Open Wednesday through Monday, 10 am to 6 pm.

<u>Admission</u>: Adults, 10 €. Additional fee for temporary exhibits. Children ages 4 to 25 (students) 7 €. Children under 3, free. Save your ticket stub for reductions on the other museums in the park.

Galerie de Paléontologie (The Museum of Paleontology) This museum houses over 650 skeletons, and several hundred species of invertebrates as well. Come see your favorite triceratops!

<u>Hours</u>: Open daily from 10 am to 6 pm except Tuesdays.

<u>Admission</u>: Adults 10 €. Children 3 to 25 and still students, 7 €. Save your ticket stub for reductions on the other museums in the park.

Galerie de Minéralogie et Géologie (The Museum of Mineralogy and Geology) Not only will you see minerals, meteorites, giant crystals, and precious stones, but you'll see an array of jewels from the collection of Louis XIV.

<u>Hours</u>: Open daily except Tuesdays from 10 am to 6 pm.

<u>Admission</u>: Adults, 7 €. Ages 3 to 25 (students), 5 €. Under 3, free. Save your ticket stub for reductions on the other museums in the park. Family tickets available.

La Galerie des Enfants (The Children's Galerie). Children will be informed and entertained by the interactive bilingual displays and exhibits.

<u>Hours</u>: Open Wednesday, weekends, and holidays from 10 am to 6 pm. Open daily except Tuesday during school holidays.

<u>Admission</u>: Adults 13 € (includes the Grande Galerie de l'Evolution), children ages 4 to 25 (students) cost 10 €.

Le Menagerie (Zoo) includes primarily small and medium-sized animals. Some of these are endangered or rare species. The zoo is involved in a breeding program that helps to preserve fragile species.

<u>Hours</u>: Open 10 am to 6 pm Monday through Saturday. Open 10 am to 6:30 pm Sundays and holidays.

<u>Admission</u>: Adults, 13 €. Children ages 4 to 25 (still students), 10 €. Age 3 and under, free.

Greenhouses (Les Grandes Serres) Open from 10 am to 6 pm. Adults, 7 €, ages 4-25, 5 €, under 3, free.

There are two restaurants on the property since it will likely take you more than a full day to see everything. You can peruse the very extensive website, which is in French, but the images should give a good idea of the vast choice of activities here. Better still, just go yourself and explore.

The Official website of the Gardens:
http://www.jardindesplantes.net
Natural History museum: https://www.mnhn.fr/en

<u>Hours:</u> The park is open from 7:30 am to 7:30 pm. In winter the hours are slightly shorter.

<u>Admission</u>: The Gardens themselves are free except the Alpine Garden, which costs 2 € on weekends. Greenhouses, 7 €. See websites for more about individual museums.

<u>Getting there</u>: 57 rue Cuvier, Paris 75005. Métro line 5 or 10, Gare d'Austerlitz. Line 10, Jussieu, Line 7, Censier Daubenton. Also RER C Gare d'Austerlitz.

Quai St. Bernard What a great place for a water-front picnic, away from the tourist crowds, with wide sidewalks and specially carved seating areas on the water's edge. Scattered around you are outdoor sculptures, but the main attraction is the Seine at one of its widest points. I love it because it seems to be a nearly undiscovered waterfront park in Paris.

Maison des Trois Thés Put wine-tasting on the back burner just a moment. Here is *the* place on the planet to taste...tea. It is the largest tea-tasting establishment in the world, not so much in the size of the building, but teas offered, 300 available for tasting, out of more than 1000 on site. The Tea Master is Maitre Tseng, who collaborates with two renowned French chefs. She is one of only ten Chinese tea masters, and the only one outside China. The art and ritual of a real tea ceremony, Gong Fu Cha, awaits you for tasting, from a large stoneware teapot heated over a flame, poured into tiny, delicate teacups. It's not just any cup of tea!

<u>Hours</u>: Open from Tuesday to Sunday from 11 am to 7:30 pm. No arrivals after 6:30 pm. Reservations recommended on Friday, Saturday, and Sunday. Please refrain from wearing strong fragrances.

<u>Cost</u>: About 20 € for the tasting.

<u>Getting there</u>: 1 rue St. Médard. Metro line 7 Place Monge. Phone: (33) 01 43 36 93 84.

My Favorites in the 5th

The 5th is one of my favorite places to wander, since there is so much to see. Here the roads are narrow and curve around to interesting destinations.

Rue Mouffetard is always lively and good for eating.

Walking everywhere in the Latin Quarter

Quai St. Bernard: For a picnic and lazy sunbath

Latin quarter: Between St. Michel and the Seine (tourist central, but fun).

Wanderings in the 5th

This walk alone takes just over 2 hours, but of course you'll want to visit, look, lunch, and dawdle along the way, so it's very elastic. You'll take longer if you do any inside visits. Places to visit include the Panthéon, the Mosque, one or more museums or the zoo at the Jardin des Plantes, or the Institut du Monde Arabe. All of these interesting sites could take you well over a full day.

1. <u>Start at St. Michel</u>. Go through the pedestrian area (the one between the river and the fountain at Place Saint Michel), where you'll find Rue de la Huchette, Rue Saint Severin, and Rue de la Harpe, and then get back out onto Rue St. Michel.

2. Go south on Boulevard St. Michel until you see La Sorbonne on your left. Stop for photos or to listen to street performers. There are also cafés in the courtyard just in front of the historic university.

3. Go to the next street down, Rue Cujas (the road just after the Sorbonne) and turn left. This will take you straight to the Panthéon.

4. Next to that you'll see the Eglise St. Etienne du Mont. Do go inside, it's lovely. Then outside again, go around the right side (facing) and scoot along the Rue Clovis (named after the first king of France.)

5. When you reach Rue Descartes, go left a couple blocks or so and look around. Then turn and go the opposite direction on Descartes. Keep going. This will eventually run into the Place de la Contrescarp, a fun roundabout surrounded by cafés and ambiance, then the road will turn into Rue Mouffetard.

6. Linger down the Rue Mouffetard, until you get to the Rue de L'Epée de Bois as you go towards the mosque (details above). Do a visit if you like, and/or circle around the building and have tea or cous cous.

7. Then almost directly across the street (Rue Geoffroy Saint Hilaire) you'll see the Jardin des Plantes. Here there are many gardens inside one big area, plus several museums, restaurants, and a zoo.

8. Toward the opposite end of the Jardin, you'll have access (go left and walk for a few minutes on the Quai Saint Bernard) to a crossover which will lead you to the part of the Quai St. Bernard that overlooks the Seine.

9. The next bridge, Pont de Sully, will take you back to the Ile de Saint Louis where you can get some Bertillon ice cream, or walk around the island.

Keep going and you'll hit Métro station Sully-Moreland, line 7.

Paris 6th

The sixth district is chic and classy, lively and artistic. The Saint Germain Church and surrounding area are soaked in history. You won't want to miss it. Where should I begin? With the biggest attraction in this neighborhood, the Garden of Luxembourg.

Main Sights in the 6th

Garden of Luxembourg is the second largest park in Paris and is a majestic stretch of varied spaces: groomed green lawns surrounding statues and flowers, with chairs scattered on gravel walkways; wooded groves where you can sit and read or picnic or listen to summer concerts (and sometimes even do ballroom dancing.) You'll see fountains, palm trees, large walks, tennis courts, pony rides and the imposing Luxembourg palace, home of the French senate. The centerpiece is an octagonal pond with a simple fountain spurting upward while miniature sailboats glide across its surface. All around are stunning explosions of color in flower gardens that are carefully designed and planted (several times per year) to be a feast for the eyes.

Close to the Rue Vaugirard entrance is the Medici Fountain, which is a work of art, not just the statue, but the whole scene. It's a shady, peaceful place to park yourself and read or picnic. Across the park and past the fountain you'll find pony rides for small children, tennis courts, live entertainment at certain times, and an ample supply of enamel painted metal chairs surrounding the flower beds and fountains. A small café under the trees will provide you with ice cream, snacks, and other refreshments.

Getting there: The Luxembourg Gardens have several entrances. The easiest way to get there is to take the RER B to the Luxembourg stop. Exit the station following the signs to Luxembourg Gardens (Jardin du Luxembourg) and it leads you directly to the main entrance.

Just outside the gate you may have the opportunity to buy roasted chestnuts in winter or, in summer, ice cream from a vendor who sells close to 50 flavors. (I haven't counted them, but there are a lot, including chocolate orange, my favorite, and lavender, which I haven't had the nerve to sample.) Once inside, wander freely. There are maps posted here and there, so you can't get lost. And of course, you won't be alone. It's one of the most crowded parks in the city.

Rue Bucci is a lively pedestrian road extending from St. André des Arts, just southwest of St. Michel, and intersecting with Rue de la Seine, which leads, as you might guess, north to the Seine River. Along Rue de la

Seine you'll see restaurants, chic clothing stores and some art galleries.

Getting there: If you take RER B to St. Michel or Métro line 4 to St. Michel, you can start at Saint André des Arts and continue straight from there.

Worth Seeing in 6th

St. Michel and Rue St. André des Arts The St. Michel area straddles the 5th and 6th districts and is just south of the Seine River in the middle of the city. (See the 5th for more on the fountain.) Just beyond and to the right (as you face the fountain) you'll see the pedestrian road, St. André des Arts, which connects further down to Rue Bucci. Like Bucci, it is flanked by restaurants and shops and filled with strolling tourists.

Getting there: Métro line 4, St. Michel.

Pont des Arts A pedestrian bridge linking the 6th district and the Louvre. It's great for picnics, strolling, and relaxing in the sun. There used to be padlocks attached to the railing, supposedly accompanied by wishes. At one time part of the railing broke and the mayor was not happy about it. The practice of attaching padlocks, however, didn't stop. You'll see plenty of them on the railing near the Square du Vert Galant, on the western tip of the Ile de la Cité.

St. Sulpice Church and surrounding area This is the second largest Catholic church in Paris, after Notre Dame. The current building was erected in 1631 on top of a previous church from the 13th century. In recent times this church became better-known following the publication of the novel The Da Vinci Code, which featured the church in the story. The pipe organ has been called the most beautiful sounding organ in the world and has welcomed many renowned organists over the years. There are frequent concerts on Sundays after Mass. In front of the church is a beautiful large fountain with statues of four bishops. Open 7:30 am to 7:30 pm.

Getting there: Line 4 Métro to St. Sulpice or Line 10 to Métro Mabillon.

Art Galleries Wander all around the Rue de Seine, Rue Jacob, and Rue Mazarine. See also special categories section, page 229.

My Favorites in 6th

St. André des Arts, St. Michel and surrounding areas.

St. Germain Area Wandering: one of my favorite neighborhoods for wandering. Follow the walking route suggested below.

Jardin du Luxembourg: I could hang out here all day on a nice day, and I especially love the Medici Fountain. Be sure to have a look. It's idyllic.

A Neighborhood Wandering in the 6th (St Germain des Prés)

1. <u>Start at Odeon</u> (Métro line 4, Odéon). Look for the 18th century street, Cours du Commerce St. André across Saint Germain. Cut straight through, but pause to observe the cafés and shops, as well as a restaurant called Le Procope. This is Paris' oldest café (founded in 1686), where Ben Franklin and Voltaire philosophized.

2. Exit the narrow courtyard and turn left on Ave. St. André, continuing straight until it becomes Rue Bucci. (You may wish to hang around here a bit before continuing on. You'll see why when you get there!) Cross Rue de Seine and your next right will be Rue Bourbon le Chateau, a very short road.

3. Cross over Rue de l'Echaudé and turn right on Rue de Furstenberg. This road also is not very long, but it's scenic, with a large tree in the center of the road. Not far from here (at # 7) is a small boutique, La Maison du Choux, dedicated to choux pastry (small puffs filled with cream). Last time I was there they ran out of 150 of them in

about 15 minutes. When I finally got mine, they were yummy. Also, on Furstenberg at # 6 is the museum of artist Eugene Delacroix. The museum is open daily from 9:30 to 5:30, except Tuesdays. Admission 7 €. Under age 18 free, European Union residents under 26, free.

4. Continue to Rue Jacob and turn left. On Rue Jacob you'll find antique shops and some art galleries. Composer Richard Wagner and French authors Jean Racine and Colette lived on this road.

5. Continue straight to Bonaparte, go left, then left again on St. Germain. The area around the church is animated with cafés, street musicians, and crowds. The church itself, founded in the 6th century A.D., was originally a kind of fortress including an abbey, built outside the original Paris city walls.

6. Go west then on St. Germain and turn down Rue du Dragon, for more quaintness and eating possibilities. At Carrefour de la Croix Rouge, turn left up Rue du Four. Feel free to wander right down Rue des Canettes or Rue Princesse, either of which will take you to the St. Sulpice neighborhood. Existentialists Sartre, De Beauvoir, and Camus hung out in this neighborhood with other bohemians at Café de

Flore and Les Deux Magots, two historic and celebrated establishments. French writers Balzac and Racine lived in this area on Rue Visconti.

The Northeast

Districts 3, 10, 18, 19, 20

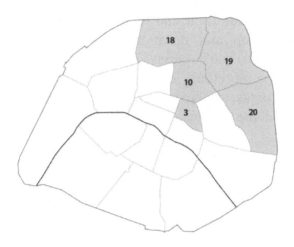

Northeast

This section of your journey encompasses 5 districts in the northeast of Paris. You'll likely find yourself breathing a sigh of relief as the crowds thin down mostly to locals, and the noise settles to a normal city purr. Still, there is plenty of activity here. Parisians frequent the

Marchés and design boutiques of the 3rd, stroll the canals of the 10th and 19th, or amble among the gravestones of the famous at Père Lachaise Cemetery in the 20th.

Even in the 18th, once you've admired Sacré Coeur, the basilica, and its crowded, bohemian surroundings, you'll find upscale mansions, winding streets, and bustling commerce on Rue Lepic and Rue des Abbesses, and so many steps up and down terraced walkways and stairways that you'll surely have your exercise. A kaleidoscope of ethnic diversity, tree-lined avenues leading to parks, smaller but worthwhile museums, and of course all the intangible French flavor you've enjoyed up to now.

Each of the five districts covered in this section has a unique personality and atmosphere. When I think of the 3rd, I think of the village-like mood of the narrow streets. In the 10th, it's canals and bridges, and of course, Indian food! In the 18th, you can't miss Sacré Coeur and Montmartre and all its busy energy, both ethnic and artistic. In the 19th are several fantastic parks and majestic tree-lined avenues. In the 20th, an artsy, bohemian village feel. Does that whet your appetite to go experience them for yourself?

You may wish to start in the 3rd district and merge northward into the 10th. If you go this way, east from the 3rd across the Place de la République, you can follow the Canal Saint Martin northward, and you'll be in the 10th in an effortless transition. If you keep going north, you'll end up in the 19th still alongside the Canal. From there, you target the parks in the 19th, or head west to the 18th and Montmartre.

This section won't have many "main" attractions from tourist books, but plenty of "life Paris". You won't get bored. Promise!

Sacré Coeur Basilica in the 18th

Paris 3rd

Worth Seeing in the 3rd

Place de la République This enormous crossroads brings together the edges of the 3rd, the 10th, and the 11th districts. It was completely renovated in 2013, going from a busy thoroughfare with cars shooting in all directions around the grand statue to a wide paved square. Here you can sit around the fountain or on one of the red metal chairs scattered about for your use. It's a gathering place and a stop-and-rest place. Where else would you be perfectly safe in the middle of a big intersection?

Musée des Arts et Métiers The best way to think of this is a museum of industry and progress. Here you'll find the first mechanical calculator created by Blaise Pascal, early airplane models, early instruments of all kinds, like binoculars, cameras, cars, as well as each successive and more perfected version of it. It's absolutely fascinating, especially for those who like inventions and mechanical devices. These you'll find in seven categories: Scientific Instruments, materials, mechanics, transportation, energy, construction, and communication. The museum was established in 1794, as a repository of these signs of inventive progress through history.

Hours: Tuesday through Thursday, open 10 am to 6 pm; Friday open 10 am to 9 pm. Saturday and Sundays, open 10 am to 6 pm. Closed Mondays.

Admission: 8 € for adults; Under 18, free. Free to E. U. residents up to age 26. Temporary exhibits, add 6 €. Free the first Sunday of the month and Fridays from 6 pm to 9 pm; included in the Museum Pass.

https://www.arts-et-metiers.net/musee/visitor-information

Getting there: Take Métro line 3 to the station Arts et Métiers. You'll see the museum as soon as you get out of the Métro, or soon thereafter

Le Marché des Enfants Rouges is the oldest marché in Paris, from 1615. The name comes from what was once a nearby orphanage in 1534 whose children were always dressed in red uniforms, hence the name "Les Enfants Rouges". This covered market is more than a place for veggies. There are open-air and covered restaurant stands, as well as traditional restaurants huddled so close together it's as though everyone shares in a group party. It's especially crowded on Sundays when people come for brunch. It's calmer in the afternoons, so to catch the energy, come in the mornings. Things wind down around 1 pm, or later on Sundays.

Hours: Open Tuesday through Saturday 8:30 am to 7:30 pm. Sunday, open 8:30 am to 2 pm.

The adjacent streets, especially Rue de Bretagne, have a village feel. Nearby you'll see "maisons de creations", which are fashion boutiques with creations of up-and-coming designers.

Getting there: Line 3 Arts et Métiers, Temple, or République are all walkable. 39 Rue de Bretagne.

Place de la République

Musée de Picasso The newly renovated museum is house in a small private chateau, the Hôtel Salé, built in 1656. It contains the world's largest collections of paintings, sculptures, and ceramics by Pablo Picasso. Come see thousands of works of the great artist...sculptures, paintings, and many other pieces from his personal archives. Picasso spent most of his life in Paris, in Montmartre and Montparnasse as well as in the south of France, where he died.

http://www.museepicassoparis.fr/

Hours: Open 10:30 am to 6 pm from Tuesday through Friday. Saturday and Sunday open 9:30 to 6 pm. Phone 01.42.71.25.21. Closed Mondays.

Admission: Adults 14 €. Audio guide: 5 €. Children under 18: free with ID. Covered by the Paris Museum Pass. Free the first Sunday of each month.

Getting there: Metro line 1 Saint-Paul, line 8 Saint-Sébastien-Froissart, line 8 Chemin Vert. The address is 5 rue de Thorigny in the 3rd.

My Favorites in the 3rd

Arts et Métiers Museum: See the description above. Allow yourself enough time to go through every floor. It's fascinating to see technical progress and inventions over the centuries to the present.

Marché des Enfants Rouges. It has a great atmosphere, especially for Sunday Brunch. I ate Moroccan specialties there with a friend. They also have French, Lebanese, Japanese, Italian, and others that you'll just have to go see . . . and taste!

Paris 10th

The Saint Martin Canal, 10th

Worth seeing in the 10th

After you've wandered around the 3rd district, try a neighborhood wandering into the 10th. The best highlight of the 10th district is the Saint Martin Canal, which runs 4.5 kilometers or about 3 miles through the 10th and 19th. A few walking options are described below. These wanderings start out the same, then at a given point you can go either east, west, or north. Details for the walk are toward the end of this section.

The Saint Martin Canal This canal runs through Paris north to south and there are also 9 locks along the way. You can watch cruise boats descend the locks, or better still, ride one yourself. The cruise company, Canauxrama, will take you through all the locks on a 2.5-hour cruise starting from either north or south. The company also does cruises on the rivers Seine and Marne. Unlike the typical Seine River cruises through central Paris (done by numerous companies), the canal cruises are quieter and slower-paced. Since the canals go outside the city, you can take cruises that go beyond the Paris city limits. Some take most of the day if that interests you. The Canauxrama website will give a full listing of tours available, in varying lengths of time and locations. www.canauxrama.com/en/ Tel. (33) 01 42 39 15 00.

You can catch the canal boat either at the northern end, at the Bassin de la Villette or the southern end, at the Port de l'Arsenal at Bastille. Reservations are necessary.

Cost is 18 € per person for the 2.5 hour Paris cruise on the St. Martin Canal. Other thematic cruises are available at different prices. Consult the website for a full listing.

Getting there: Northern access: take Metro lines 2, 5, or 7bis to Jaurès to the Bassin de la Villette. Buses lines 26 or 48. To the south, take lines 1, 5, or 8 to Bastille. Take exit Opéra or Pont de l'Arsenal. Buses 20, 29, 76, 86, 87, 91.

Gare de l'Est and the Indian and Sri Lankan community Faubourg-St. Denis, which runs north to south along the east side of the Gare du Nord, La Chapelle, and Rue de Cail.

If you're in Paris in late August and are interested in Indian culture, look for the Ganesh Festival. Ganesh is one of the deities most loved by the Indian people and is represented by an elephant head. Note: If you are alone, it's best to avoid this area after dark. (Gare de l'Est and Gare du Nord)

Getting there: Take line 2 to La Chapelle or Line 2 or RER B to Gare du Nord. (La Chapelle would be easier, since Gare du Nord is a big place and it's easy to get confused.)

A Neighborhood Wandering in the 10th

1. From the 3rd to the 10th: After your visit at the Marché des Enfants Rouge and thereabouts, continue north towards Rue du Temple towards République. Cross the big square and keep going on Rue du Faubourg du Temple just until you see the Saint Martin Canal on your left.

2. Go left on the Quai de Valmy. As you stroll along the tree-lined canal, notice the metal bridges arching across the canal (there are 9 in all), as well as the locks that are used to lower boats to the level below. If you don't see them right away, just keep walking. And don't miss them for the many trees that line either side of the canal.

3. Walk north along the canal. At the Rue de la Grange aux Belles on the right side of the canal you'll see one of the pivoting bridges, turning to let boats through. You can tell you're on a pivoting bridge if you look down and there's a metal rail crossing the bridge at either end.

   From this point you can go in three directions. East (start at #4), North (#8), or West (#10).

   To go **EAST** towards Belleville (see the 20th, later in the booklet)

4. Turn right on the Rue de la Grange aux Belles. When you reach the entrance to the Hôpital Saint-Louis, go through the doorway and cut across the grounds. (You can walk around the hospital if you prefer.) On the right you'll see the original 400-year-old hospital, and on the left, the modern version.

5. Exit at Avenue Claude Vellefaux, clear on the other side, cross the street and go up Rue Saint Marthe. Your map will help here because there are several roads that come together at the same point.

6. From Rue Saint Marthe, merge right into Rue de Sambre et Meuse, then take your right onto

Boulevard de la Villette. Continue until you reach the Métro station Belleville (This is also where you take the Rue de Belleville, *not* to be confused with the Boulevard de Belleville, which goes south) and turn left onto Rue de Belleville.

7. Wander up along this road into an ethnic and artistic haven. This will take you into the 20th. For more detailed info on the Belleville district, go just a bit further to the section on the 20th.

Another option is to head **NORTH**:

8. Keep going up the Quai de Valmy for 10 minutes or so and cross the big Rue La Fayette towards the Rotonde de la Villette, which is the entrance to the wider part of the canal. This becomes the Bassin de la Villette, and is in the 19th.

9. Wander along the wide canal and forget for a moment you're in a large European city. Here people stroll along the cobbled canal banks, enjoying the smaller crowds and the peaceful reflections on the water. There are still cafés and restaurants, and even movie theatres here, so you won't be bored or hungry.

Or you can veer towards the **WEST** towards the Gare de l'Est.

10. From the Rue de la Grange aux Belles on the left side of the canal facing north, turn left on the Rue des Récollets and you'll find the entrance to a small, charming park, Jardin Villemin. This isn't far at all from the Gare de l'Est, around which you'll find Indian and other ethnic restaurants. More Indian stores and restaurants are clustered around the Gare du Nord as well. You can also take the Métro at Gare de l'Est (lines 4, 5, and 7) if you'd like to move onto other neighborhoods.

My Favorites in the 10th

Wandering. The best thing in the 10th is wandering along the canal, enjoying the village atmosphere, strolling under the trees, across the metal footbridges, and observing the locks. They have always fascinated me, especially if a tour boat is passing through.

Paris 18th

The 18th district of Paris is probably the most visited area outside of the central area. This is due to the popularity of the famous neighborhood, Montmartre. The white dome of the Sacré Coeur Basilica dominates North Paris. The church sits on the Butte Montmartre (a butte is a high hill), Paris' highest point. At night the church is lit up, glowing white, like a sentinel watching over the northern part of the city. All around the basilica are stunning views, quaint eateries, and a concentration of artists demonstrating their skills. Yes, it's crowded with tourists, but a must-see area of northern Paris.

The name Montmartre means mountain or mound of the martyrs, after the death of Saint Denis, France's early patron saint, in 250 AD. Saint Denis was the first bishop of Lutetia (or Lutèce, the original name for Paris), and was beheaded by the Romans, who had established two temples on the hill where we now find the Basilica. According to legend, he picked up his head and walked about six miles to the town that now bears his name, Saint Denis, preaching all the way.

This was also the place of popular uprising (The Paris Commune of 1870), crushed three months later. Soon after, it became an enclave for impressionist and other well-known painters, such as Dali, Monet, Van Gogh, Modigliani, and Picasso.

Then throughout the 19th century, artists, composers, and writers flocked to Montmartre. Scattered around the winding neighborhoods you can still see the former homes of some of the impressionists, such as Modigiliani, Renoir, and Utrillo.

Main Sights in the 18th

Sacré Coeur (Sacred Heart) Basilica. This church isn't one of the oldest in Paris (1875 to 1914), but tourists flock here, not just for the church itself, but for the panoramic view of Paris on its front steps. The Neo-Roman-Byzantine architecture of Sacré Coeur is more impressive outside than inside, though there is a magnificent painting inside on the dome overhead.

To reach the basilica, you can climb up the steps that wind up either side of the grassy hill. An easier alternative would be the nearby funicular, which will take you up for one Métro ticket. Benches along the way enable you to catch your breath and catch the view at increasingly elevated stages. Then at the top, once you reach the threshold of the church and its steps, turn around and look out at the spread of Paris. There are higher views inside towers such as Montparnasse and the Eiffel Tower, but here you are outside at the city's highest natural point, with all of Paris at your feet.

Steep staircase in Montmartre

Place du Tertre Once you have visited the church, circle around to the back, and follow the crowds. You'll find yourself in a large square surrounded by shops, restaurants, and buildings. In that square are today's artists painting mostly pictures of Paris itself, to be bought by tourists like you! It's still energetic and interesting and you won't want to miss the buzz. Keep wandering, for all around you'll find interesting treasures, such as Montmartre's only vineyard, Clos Montmartre on Rue Saint Vincent, which produces around 500 liters of wine per year. In October each year there is a parade of the various growers of alcohol-destined fruit.

Getting there: Take Métro line 2 and stop at Anvers. Go towards the hillside up the Rue de Steinkurque until you see the domed church rising like a huge mirage before you.

Musée de Montmartre and Jardins Renoir Come get a glimpse of the lifestyle and flavor of this iconic and historical neighborhood at the museum and gardens. The museum resides in the 17th century Bel Air House, the oldest building in Montmartre, and formerly a gathering and studio space for impressionist painters. Outside, three gardens are dedicated to Renoir, who lived here for two years. From here you can see the Montmartre vineyard, Le Clos Montmartre.

Hours: It's open daily 10 am to 6 pm.

Admission: Adult admission is 13€ for temporary exhibits. Otherwise, 12 €. Children under 10, free. Free audioguide with entrance. Gardens only, 5 €. Covered by Museum Pass.

Getting there: 12 rue de Cortot. Take Metro line 12, Lamarck-Caulaincourt or Line 2 to Anvers then the funicular up the hill toward the Basilica.

http://www.museedemontmartre.fr/exhibitions

The café **Au Lapin Agile** is where Picasso, Utrillo, Modigliani, and other artists spent time, as well as at Le Bateau Lavoir. Today Au Lapin Agile is a cabaret, still in business at 22 Rue des Saules. A show and a drink costs

28 €. 20 € for students to age 26, except for Saturdays and holidays. Open from 9 to midnight.

After World War I, artists began to congregate in the Montparnasse neighborhoods in the south of Paris.

What some people don't know is that there are other interesting neighborhoods surrounding the basilica: to the west, Rue des Abbesses, Rue Lepic, and Rue Caulaincourt, trendy, chic, or just crowded and cute. To the east, the areas of Barbès and La Goutte d'Or fill the atmosphere with the bustle of a strong North African and African presence. Here you'll find noise, bargains, street vendors, and happy mayhem. In the 18th there is plenty to see.

Worth Seeing in the 18th

Le Moulin des Galettes was formerly a dance hall that was popular in the 19th century. The famous windmill you find there, called Blute-fin, was built in 1622 and is classified as an historic monument. It became the subject of paintings by Renoir and Van Gogh. This property was also involved in the turbulent history of the area, during the Napoleonic Wars and the Franco Prussian War. In 1830 it became a cabaret. Today a renovated Moulin de la Galette is a highly recommended restaurant with reasonable prices. www.lemoulindelagalette.fr/en/

Espace Dali: If you like surrealism and the art of Salvador Dali, this museum contains 300 of Dali's works.

It is located at 11 rue Poulbot near the Sacré Coeur Basilica. www.**daliparis**.com

Hours: Open 10 am to 6 pm. In July and August, open until 8 pm

Admission: 13 € for adults; 9 € for students and those under age 26; children under 8 free; covered by the Museum Pass. Audioguide, 3 €.

Rue Saint Vincent This steep, picturesque road joins with Rue des Saules (where you'll find Au Lapin Agile.)

Église Saint Pierre-de-Montmartre One of the oldest churches in Paris, this one dates to 1134. Find it at 2 rue du Mont-Cenis.

Specialty shopping at Barbès: One thing you'll notice as soon as you get off the Métro at Anvers is the number of small fabric shops. About two blocks from the Métro you'll see the Marché Saint Pierre, 5 stories of fabric. Along Rue Barbès you'll see discount shops, street venders, and sidewalk sales. It's not necessarily chic or well-made, but it is inexpensive.

Moulin Rouge Known around the world, this cabaret show has been around since 1889. It's situated at 82 Boulevard de Clichy. You'll be entertained in a thoroughly French experience. It won't be cheap, however. Dinner and a show can run above 200 € per person, though they also have lunch for about 165 €.

Even if you don't go, you should visit the beautiful web site. www.moulinrouge.fr/?lang=en

Le Beauvilliers at 52 Lamarck is called by the Michelin Guide the most fashionable restaurant in Montmartre. It was named after Antoine Beauvillier, a chef in the court of Louis XVIII.

Flea Market Porte de la Chapelle (Marche aux Puces de St Ouen) 18th. This is THE flea market of Paris, and it's the largest antiques market in the world, including 7 different markets. Some of these are covered and others are in open air. It was established in 1870 and today hosts over 1900 merchants. Open Saturday 11-6, Sunday 10-6, and Monday 11 to 5 pm.

Getting there: Métro line 4 Porte de Clignancourt or Line 13 Garibaldi. http://www.pucesparis.com/

Paris Flea Market

My Favorites in the 18th

I like the wandering neighborhoods (are you surprised?) the best. Strolling through Rue des Abbesses and onto the tree-lined avenues of Caulaincourt is a peaceful but foot-moving experience. I could easily spend a day just hanging out there, watching shoppers, street entertainment, visiting boutiques and tiny lunch places.

A Neighborhood Wandering in the 18th

1. Explore the area to the west of the Sacré Coeur. From Sacré Coeur or walk (or ride) to Métro Pigalle and cross the street north to Houdon.

2. Go to Rue des Abbesses and turn left. Here you'll find a very lively commercial street with plenty of busy atmosphere, shops, restaurants, and a narrow, cobbled road winding like it has for centuries. Just on your right is the Abbesses Métro stop, which has the first-ever in Paris art-deco design. This was originally near the Hotel de Ville then moved to its present location.

3. Go up Rue des Abbesses towards the west. As it forks, keep left on the Rue Lepic. It will curve to the right and snake back east. Look for Rue Girardon and go left. Go left again at Impasse Girardon and notice how you feel like you're in an upscale neighborhood. This road turns into Avenue Junot, which has lovely private homes

and artists' studios. At the end of this road is Rue Caulaincourt, a shady, curving tree-lined street with an upper-class ambiance.

4. Turn left on Tourlaque and keep bearing right until it becomes Rue des Abbesses again. This will lead you back to Houden where you turn right and find yourself once again at Pigalle.

5. If you'd like to continue on . . . See the neighborhood of Pigalle. Most people think of the red-light district, but honestly, I've never seen a prostitute in the daytime in this area. It's known for many other things. For example, if you're a musician in need of equipment this is your neighborhood, with various shops to browse. Otherwise, just go down Pigalle (you're now in the 9th) left on Victor Masse, right on R. H. Monnier. On your left you'll see Place Gustave Toudouze, a shady cutaway from the main road with several outdoor cafés under the trees.

6. Turn left on Rue Notre Dame de Lorette, which eventually leads to Place Saint George, a picturesque square, and continuing on, to the church Notre Dame de Lorette, where both Georges Bizet and Claude Monet were baptized. Here you can take the Métro by the same name (line 7) and head towards Châtelet if you want to get back to central Paris. If you'd rather shop,

keep going until you reach Rue La Fayette and turn right.

7. Keep going and you'll eventually hit the huge department stores, Galleries Lafayette and Printemps on your right, and not very far to your left is the Opéra Garnier.

Paris 19th

In the 19th there are three main attractions you will want to see. In addition to these you'll enjoy a neighborhood wanderings around Rue Botzaris and Rue Manin, along lovely curved streets overshadowed with trees and surrounding the Park Buttes Chaumont. To the east of the park are clusters of streets filled with individual houses, rather rare in Paris. You do find them hidden away in particular neighborhoods, though the vast majority of dwellings are apartments.

Main Sights in the 19th

Parc Buttes Chaumont This lovely park was created from an area that was a refuse site and a quarry, upon which little would grow. Now there are grassy hills everywhere surrounding a manmade lake complete with a waterfall. Picnic on the grass, jog or walk on its paved paths, and enjoy the waterfall or the lake.

<u>Getting there</u>: The best way to get there is on the line 7b, one of the smallest metro lines of Paris. You can reach it by first taking the line 2 to Jaurès then go direction Pré St. Gervais on the line 7b. Get out at station Botzaris or Buttes Chaumont.

Parc de La Villette This is a totally different kind of park than the one you just read about, the largest (136 acres) and most unusual inside Paris. It contains the largest science museum in Europe, with regular conferences and special exhibits (see below.) There is also a science library and planetarium, a special theatre called la Géode that shows IMAX and other 3D films, all in the same complex. A massive concert hall, a symphony hall, and a music conservatory (and nearby Musée de la Musique, described below) reside on its perimeter.

In the park itself are 12 different gardens, including a bamboo garden, dune garden, garden of the dragon, with an 80-foot steel dragon kids can play upon. Sculptures can be large and weird, such as that representing a huge bicycle buried in the ground. https://lavillette.com/en/ And of course, playing fields as well.

Here you can enjoy all kinds of festivals and expositions, as well as open-air events (films, concerts, dance) in La Grande Halle, formerly used to auction cattle. Through all of this variety runs the Canal de l'Ourq, a waterway that branches off of the Bassin de la Villette (see following.)

<u>Hours</u>: Open daily 9:30 am to 6:30 pm.

<u>Getting there</u>: Take Métro line 7 to Porte de La Villette, or line 5 to Porte de Pantin. The tramway 3b will also take you directly to Porte de la Villette.

Cité des Sciences et de l'Industrie, or Science and Industry Museum, is the largest of its kind in Europe. Space and the universe are the themes of Explora, on the first two levels of this interactive museum. Some themes include the brain, light games, energy, transportation, and genetics. On the north second floor mezzanine is the Planétarium. Here you can either take a trip to the stars or journey through the human body! <u>www.cite-sciences.fr/en/home</u>

A second "museum within a museum" is **Cité des Enfants** on the ground floor. There is one section for children ages 2 to 7, and another ages 5 to 12. There are six themed zones where children can interact and learn and a special exhibit of baby animals as well. Sessions are 1 ½ hours long. Reservations are recommended, especially during school holidays.

The third main section of the museum is called **La Géode**. It shows movies inside a huge steel globe (118 feet) that can be seen all over the park. Films are about science and culture and include IMAX productions.

In the same vicinity outside of the museum is the Argonaut, a 1957 submarine, is available for visits for 3

€; (see hours below.) The Cinaxe is also nearby. This simulator allows up to 56 people to experience a film sequence in real life, such as a flight through the skies or a race. 3-D glasses and hydraulic seats add to the realism. About 5 € for a 15-minute experience.

There are restaurants and snack bars inside the museum, as well as all around the neighborhood.

<u>Hours</u>: The Explora Museum is open from Tuesday to Saturday, 10 am to 6 pm. Sundays, 10 am to 7 pm. La Géode is open Tuesday to Sunday from 10:30 to 8:30 pm, with shows hourly. The Argonaut Submarine is open from Tuesday to Saturday from 10 am to 6 pm, and Sunday until 7 pm.

<u>Admission</u>: Individual tickets combine the Planetarium, the Argonaut, and the Museum, permanent and temporary exhibits; *reservations are required at the time of this writing*. Adults 12 €. Under age 25, 9 €. Under 6, free. Cite des Enfants tickets: 12€.

Musée de la Musique Come walk through the history of music with an audio-visual experience featuring 1000 musical instruments on exhibit in the permanent collection, out of a total of 7000. These instruments date from the 16th century to the present day. Non-European music is included in the collection. You can also see instruments owned and played by such historical greats as Chopin and Berlioz, as well as by contemporary musicians such as Frank Zappa.

The museum is located inside the Cité de la Musique, which is a conservatory for dance and music (The Paris National Conservatory of Music and Dance.) They also host a variety of music concerts throughout the year. The concert hall and museum are on the eastern side of the immense building. It was redesigned by the acclaimed architect, Jean Nouvel in 2015. The building alone is worth a view. The rooftop view is accessible to the public.

Hours: Open Tuesday through Friday from 12 noon to 6 pm; Saturday and Sunday 10 am to 6 pm. Closed Mondays.

Admission: Adults, 9 € for permanent exhibits (self-guided tour), 11 € for temporary exhibits. Under age 6, free. Reduced price categories: Temporary exhibits 6 € for self-guided tours. 8 € for guided tours and includes the permanent collection. This museum is included in the Paris Pass.

Getting there: Address is 221 Ave. Jean Jaurès. Métro line 5 Porte de Pantin.

For more information on the Cité de la Musique, including concerts, and the Musée de la Musique, consult the website.

https://philharmoniedeparis.fr/en/musee-de-la-musique

Park de la Villette and Science Museum

Bassin de la Villette You've already read about and perhaps visited the part of this canal where the locks take boats from one level to another. Here is the upper part of the canal, called the Bassin de la Villette. The waterway widens and you feel like you're at a lake surrounded by Parisian apartments and tree-covered cobbled walkways. It's peaceful and beautiful, calmer than the center of the city, but still with plenty to do. Each side of the canal is lined with eateries and movie theatres.

<u>Getting there</u>: Take the Métro line 2, 5, or 7 to Stalingrad and walk toward the water.

My Favorites in the 19th

Butte Chaumont Park and surrounding neighborhoods.

Bassin de la Villette canal area as well, on a sunny day for a quiet canal-side stroll.

Paris 20th

This district is one of the biggest in Paris, and one of the last to be annexed into the city. Before that it and others were villages, among them Belleville, Saint Blaise, and Charonne. This district contains one of the most artsy, ethnic communities, Belleville, which is a neighborhood straddling both the 19th and 20th districts. There is a distinctly bohemian and artistic flavor in the 20th. Like many formerly working-class neighborhoods, this area is gradually mounting up to trendy and "bobo" (bohemian-bourgeois), though it used to be, and to some extent still is, one of the more affordable areas in Paris.

Main Sights in the 20th

Cimitière Père Lachaise The Père Lachaise Cemetery, created by Napoleon, is well-known among tourists, for its celebrated "clientele", mostly artists, writers, and statesmen. Here you'll find the who's who among the deceased, such as Chopin, Jim Morrison, Oscar Wilde, Sarah Bernhardt, Maria Callas, Edith Piaf, and impressionist painters Pissaro and Modigliano. The cemetery is the largest in Paris and perhaps the most visited in the world. There are over one million people buried there, and the cemetery was enlarged 5 times.

<u>Getting there</u>: Take Métro line 2 to Père Lachaise or Philippe August. The cemetery is free and opens at 8 am until 5:30 or 6, depending on the season.

Worth Seeing in the 20th

Belleville Community Belleville was a village on the outskirts of Paris proper until 1860. By the time of its annexation, it was the 13th largest city in France, in population. The peasants that used to occupy the hillsides moved away and in came the artists, shopkeepers, and retired folks coming from Paris to seek fresh air. Belleville has always attracted many cultures, from its early days. Part of the reason may be to work in the nearby quarry, which later became the Butte Chaumont Park. Artisans from Italy, Russia, and Greece came to work in the vast number of small shops. They kept coming in waves, Jews (eastern Europe and North Africa) in the 1960s, Asians in the 1980s, and Pakistanis in the 90s. When Belleville was finally incorporated into Paris, it was divided between 2 arrondissments, the 19th and 20th, in an effort to weaken the feisty population.

Nowadays the words that come to mind are still ethnic, bohemian, and artistic. Here is the second largest Chinatown in Paris, after one in the 13th. Belleville has the largest concentration of artists in Europe, and you see the evidence of this everywhere, with galleries and workshops scattered about. Each year in late May, there is a "Portes Ouvertes", or open house where artists open their studios for people to come and see their work and sometimes see *them* work. Belleville can be a good place to shop, depending on what you are looking for. There are a lot of Asian shops and restaurants to choose from. For a unique lunch, ever tried grilled ravioli? At Restaurant Ravioli that's almost all they serve. 47 rue de Belleville.

Getting there: Be careful to look for the Rue de Belleville, not the Boulevard de Belleville, which intersects the Rue and runs north to south. Take Métro line 2 to Belleville station. Look for Rue de Belleville and follow it east. On the other side of the intersection the road changes names to Temple, so no way to make a mistake.

Parc de Belleville Another park! This one is different from all the others mentioned, because it is small but terraced, and has a lovely overlook of the city of Paris at its highest level, near the main entrance. There are fountains here too, wooded paths and benches, and grassy picnic areas. Paris has so many gorgeous parks, you really ought to plan a few picnics into your schedule.

Getting there: Take Métro 11 to station Pyrénées for the main entrance. Another entrance is line 2, Couronnes.

La Bellevilloise In 1877 this building was the city's first worker's co-op. Since 2005 it's been an eclectic leisure and art destination, with a bar, a restaurant, art exhibits, and a concert space all under one roof. You can hear some up-and-coming bands here, and enjoy Sunday brunch and live jazz at the Halle aux Oliviers. Enjoy views from the terrace or a massage in a deck chair on the upper level.

Brunch price: Brunch and live jazz concert, 29 €. Children under 12, 13 €.

https://www.labellevilloise.com/jazz-brunch-dimanches-jours-feries/

Getting there: The address is 19-21 Rue Boyer in the 20th. Métro line 2, Ménilmontant.

The Southeast
Districts 11th, 12th, 13th

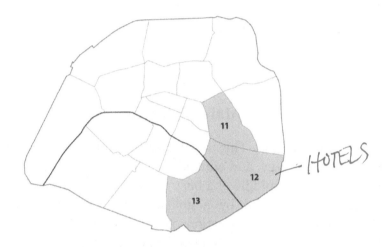

HOTELS

Southeast

The southeast sector of Paris is residential, but there are still places to draw your interest. Three districts, the 11th, the 12th, and 13th, converge here, each one with its distinctive personality. In the 11th you'll find the Place de la Bastille and its lively surroundings. The Place is the former location of the events that triggered the French Revolution. The 12th is what I call the garden of Paris, my favorite place to live. It boasts wide, shady avenues, wooded running paths, and lovely parks. Lacking specific tourist magnets, it breathes calm and beauty in every street and cobbled pathway. Further south in the 13th you encounter Chinatown, along with a quirky, fun neighborhood filled with narrow streets and alleyways, college students, and cute eateries. There's plenty to explore off the beaten path.

Paris 11th

The Main Sights in the 11th

Bastille area This area will make your head spin with noise, energy, and animation. The monument shoots up out of the middle of a busy roundabout, a thin, graceful column topped by a golden winged being. Zipping around it in all directions is the constant flow of traffic through the roundabout and along the connected streets. As you leave the Métro, there are many exits. The choice you make will lead you to one of several interesting destinations on either side of the roundabout. If you take Rue de la Roquette, you'll be on a corner covered with bars and cafés. Nearby there is an Amorino's ice cream shop you won't want to miss.

Rue de Lappe If you go down Rue de la Roquette and turn right at the Rue de Lappe, you will be on a pedestrian street hemmed on either side with restaurants and bars. You can choose a meal from Corsican, Spanish,

Auvergnat (a region close to the center of France), as well as a variety of others. Evenings are lively, for eating and/or partying after hours.

Opéra Bastille On the other hand, if you exit the Métro and follow signs for the Opéra Bastille, you'll come face to face with the modern mirrored opera house, one of the two primary opera establishments in Paris. (The other is the famous Opéra Garnier.) Check their programs here: https://www.operadeparis.fr/en/l-opera-de-paris/l-opera-bastille

Just in front of the opera house is a **restaurant/café**, *Les Grandes Marches*, which has been in Paris for quite a while, and renovated in 2012. Opera-goers, tourists, and Parisians can eat traditional French meals or seafood until 1 am. Their hot chocolate is very good. The atmosphere is elegant and relaxed at the same time.

Opéra Bastille

The Place de la Bastille Monument marks the spot where a 14th century prison called La Bastille was torn down in 1789 by an angry mob. Of course, the prison is no longer there, although some of the stones were repurposed for bridges later, and others saved for souvenirs. The few prisoners inside were released and the jailers were beheaded in a frenzy. This was the first of many violent events to come during the French Revolution. The winged statue that occupies the former location of the Bastille prison actually commemorates another event, a later revolution of 1830 and the victims of that conflict, whose names are inscribed on the Corinthian column. Atop the column is the golden "Spirit of Liberty".

Getting there: Bastille is an important stop on Métro lines 1, 5, and 8.

Worth Seeing in the 11th

Neighborhood wandering Saunter up Rue Beaumarchais (leads north to Place de la République) or Richard Lenoir (leads north all the way to the St. Martin canal) for a shady stroll.

Oberkampf is a trendy neighborhood (it's been called "shabby-chic", and you are likely to see both shabby and chic) with restaurants and ambiance. There is a Métro stop on line 5 and line 9 by the name Oberkampf.

Rue Faubourg St. Antoine A wide, busy shopping street that runs from Bastille all the way eastward to Place de la Nation. Particularly between Métro Faidherbe (halfway to Nation) and Bastille you can get some cute French clothing and other items at fair prices in boutiques and chain clothing stores (Camaiu, Naf Naf, Etam.) There is a Monoprix, if you need food or other supplies for your picnic. There are several restaurants and bars as well.

Not far from there, close to the Saint Antoine Hospital, is Rue d'Aligre. Follow this road and you'll run into the Marché d'Aligre, reputed to be one of the most reasonably-priced marchés in town. They only sell produce and plants, not meats or fish, though there is also a fish market in a storefront nearby. On weekends you'll find clothes and practical or artistic items, as well as a lively shopping vibe. Locals come here often. Unlike most French marchés, which are held once or twice per week, the Marché d'Aligre is active every day of the week except Monday. Rue du Faubourg Saint Antoine cuts a line between the 11th and 12th, and the Marché is situated in the 12th.

Port de l'Arsenal Head this way for a sleepy canal walk, which is fun but a bit hidden. Go towards the big empty plaza one street from the Opéra. Go down the sidewalk to the left of the plaza until you see a set of cobbled steps leading down towards the canal. This is the last section of the St. Martin Canal (the one you may have seen in the 19th and the 10th.) You can take or get off of the canal tour boat here too.

Nearby at a restaurant called Le Grand Bleu, you can eat seafood or have a drink at one of the café tables under the trees, or under the sun as you overlook the canal and private house boats. Pleasure boats (over 100 of them) are also moored along either side of the canal. The cobbled sidewalk is perfect for strolling. On a hillside above, you'll find grassy patches and benches and a tiny floral park. It's calm and quiet, and the reflection on the water can just lull you into a nap if you're not careful.

Musée Edith Piaf See the small apartment where the singer lived for a while. You'll see portraits and memorabilia from her life. Admission is free, though donations are welcome.

Getting there: 5 rue Crespin du Gast, 11th district. Métro line 2, Ménilmontant.

My Favorites in the 11th

The canal at the Port de l'Arsenal is my favorite place in the 11th. What a peaceful calm getaway, where you can lick an Amorino's ice cream cone or get an early tan or simply read under a tree while you listen to the lapping of the canal waters.

Restaurants to try in the 11th

One of the restaurants owned by celebrity chef Cyril Lignac, called **Le Chardenoux**, is worth a visit. Small and quaint, yet the food is elegant and delicious. 1 rue Jules Valles. Métro line 9, Rue de Boulet or Charonne. Open every day. (33) 01 43 71 49 52.

Chez Paul has served traditional French cuisine since 1900. You'll find its wonderfully refined taste at 13 rue de Charonne. Phone: (33)01 47 00 34 57. Open every day for both lunch and dinner.

Paris 12th

I call this district the garden of Paris, since much of it is green and residential, and there are several fabulous parks there. I lived on the edge of the 12th for 5 years and would go back anytime! This arrondissment has about everything, busy shopping areas like Place de la Nation, vast green spaces like Bois de Vincennes, small boutiques like *autrefois*, (in the old days) that sell bread and pastry, meat, fish, cheeses, and flowers, and bi-weekly open markets. There are several important hospitals in the 12th, as well as the Gare de Lyon, a major train station taking passengers to the Loire Valley and onward to the south of France.

Main Sights in the 12th

Nation The area called Nation is a major thoroughfare, with four Métro lines and the RER A taking you or transferring you about anywhere in the city. Despite this criss-cross of people at all times of the day, Nation remains primarily a residential area. Of course, there are shops, restaurants, a branch of the large department store chain, Printemps, and about everything else you'd need here, but not as many tourists as in the central part of the city.

The Place de la Nation is a large roundabout that surrounds a statue called The Triumph of the Republic. The original name was Place du Trône (or throne), in honor of the arrival of King Louis XIV after his marriage. Later during the Revolution, the name was sarcastically changed to "Le trône renversé", or the overturned throne, and of course you know the events that followed this description. A guillotine was set up in the Place, as well as other areas around Paris. Hundreds lost their lives there and are buried nearby in the Picpus Cemetery. The Place was renamed Nation in 1880 and the statue was established in 1889 to commemorate the one-hundredth anniversary of the revolution. Today it's a popular place for demonstrations, as is Place de la République.

Not far from the roundabout you can see two enormous columns topped with statues, one of Louis IX and the other Philippe II. This was formerly the eastern entrance into the city and tolls were collected here.

Nation is the biggest center in the 12th. It borders the 11th. Other areas in the 12th have large avenues as well, such as the Daumesnil area, with the Place Felix Eboué and its lovely fountain.

<u>Getting there</u>: Take metro lines 1, 2, 6, or 9 or the RER A to Nation.

Place de la Nation

Bercy In the 19th century, Bercy was the biggest market for wholesale wine and spirits for Parisians. At the time the village of Bercy wasn't part of Paris, so didn't have to pay the city tax. It was, however, plagued by fires and floods several times throughout the century. Bercy was annexed by Paris in 1860, and the wine trade declined in the 1950s, as wines were increasingly distributed from their regions of production. In this area there are several sites of interest (below).

Getting there: Métro line 6 to Bercy.

Bercy Park Hands down, the loveliest park in all of Paris. That's my opinion, of course. There are many runners-up, such as Monceau to the north (coming later) and Luxembourg, which you have read about. This long, rectangular park runs along the Seine River to the southeast. It has three sections, or you could say two different styles with one of them divided by the Rue Joseph Kessel.

If you come to Métro Bercy on lines 6 or 8, the thing you can't miss is an enormous stadium whose outer walls are covered with grass. This is the Palais Omnisports de Paris-Bercy, where concerts, conventions, sporting events and all sorts of entertainment happens. From there going southeast on the Rue de Bercy you'll see the first part of Bercy Park proper to your right, a large grassy park with wide open space where you can picnic or play soccer or badminton. On the side closest to the river an interesting stairway-fountain leads up to a pedestrian bridge (you'll see it when you reach the top) where you can walk across the Seine and over into the 13th.

If you continue straight through the park you pass through a gate to the second area of the park, called the

Jardin Yitzhak Rabin. An idyllic, artfully created space awaits you, with flower gardens, a rose arbor and grape arbor, benches scattered beneath the sun, a small man-made canal covered by trellises, and plenty of green space to lounge about. A footbridge will take you over top of the street to the continuation of the park, the canal, and the pond where it ends.

Bercy Village Keep going from the park (above) through another gate and you'll find yourself here in this fun, chic center, converted from former wine depots. There are still railroad tracks embedded in the cobblestones, where they used to cart in barrels of St. Emilion wine and store it in warehouses now converted into shops and restaurants. There are a Monoprix grocery store and a UGC movie theater at opposite ends of the village. Often in summer you can hear weekly or bi-weekly concerts in the cobbled courtyard of the enclosed space.

Getting there: Métro line 14 Cours St. Émilion or you can take line 6 to Bercy and walk through the park to get there.

Bercy Village

Worth Seeing in the 12th

Bois de Vincennes and Parc Floral The Parc Floral lies inside the Bois de Vincennes, which is Paris' largest public park. The Bois was a hunting ground for the Emperor Louis Napoleon. Today his chateau still stands in the city of Vincennes and is open for visits.

Though both the Bois and the Parc Floral (below) lie outside of the péripherique, they are still considered part of Paris and part of the 12th. The Bois de Vincennes is a huge, wooded area where you might want to bike, walk, or picnic. On a smaller scale, a couple of places worth seeing *inside* the Bois are the Lac de Daumesnil and the

Parc Floral (see next page.) Le Lac de Daumesnil is a man-made lake with a walking path all around, ducks and boats, and a man-made mountain in the middle, close to the Porte Dorée. Nearby there is a zoo, reopened in 2014 following renovations, as well as the Château de Vincennes.

Getting there: take line 8 to the Porte Dorée on the southeast edge of the city and you'll find the Lac de Daumesnil. You can also get there by following the Avenue Daumesnil eastward.

Musée National de l'Histoire d'Immigration Paris has a rich history of immigration and this museum tells the story. The museum is housed in the Palais de la Porte Dorée, which was built in 1931 for the World Fair of 1931. The museum surveys 200 years of immigration in France from historical, anthropological, and artistic viewpoints, with three collections following these themes. There are also temporary exhibits. Now the Immigration Museum shares this building with the Tropical Aquarium (see below.)

Hours: Open Tuesday to Friday from 10 am to 5:30 pm and Saturday and Sunday from 10 am to 7 pm.

Admission: At the time of this writing, the permanent exhibits are closed for renovation until Spring 2023. Adults 8 € for temporary exhibits. Under age 26, free.

Free the first Sunday of each month. Covered by the Museum Pass. Combined ticket with the aquarium, 12 €.

<u>Getting There</u>: Take the Métro line 8 to Porte Dorée (direction Créteil) or Tram 3a Porte Dorée. Follow the row of palm trees toward the majestic palace. It is across a large avenue from the Lac de Daumesnil part of the Bois de Vincennes. Address: 293 Avenue Daumesnil.

Aquarium Tropicale Opened in 1931, the Tropical Aquarium houses 500 species of tropical fish in 84 aquariums. There are both permanent and temporary exhibits, as well as conferences and debates. A guided visit is available on Wednesdays at 3:30 pm and Saturday/Sunday at 10:45 in May and June.

<u>Hours</u>: Tuesday to Friday from 10 am to 5:30 pm and Saturday and Sunday from 10 to 7 pm. Closed Mondays.

<u>Admission</u>: Adults 8 €. Combination ticket (Billet Palais) with the Museum of Immigration is available for 12 €. Reservations are necessary.

<u>Getting there</u>: See directions (above) for the Museum of Immigration. They are in the same building, le Palais de la Porte Dorée.

The Parc Floral is one of two major botanical gardens of Paris, containing around 3,000 types of plants. This enclosed park has many interesting (labeled) plant varieties, a man-made lake and fountain, a concert band shell with jazz concerts every weekend in June through August, and classical concerts each weekend of September. At the far end of the park, you'll find a large children's play area with rides, swings, see-saws, you name it. Each year annual competitions for dahlias and tulips are held, as well as special expositions of peonies and bonsais.

Admission: Entrance is free from October 1 to March 31. From June 1 to September 30, 2€50. Children under 7 are free. On Wednesdays there are often special children's activities. Some amusements in the play area cost extra.

Getting there: take the Métro line 1 east all the way to the end, direction Chateau de Vincennes. Exit at toward the Parc Floral sign and follow the sidewalk with the Château de Vincennes along your right side. You'll find the entrance to the Parc at the end of the sidewalk.

Cinémathèque Française This is a Museum of the Cinema, and the unique building itself is of architectural interest, designed by Frank Gehry. This is the place for cinema-lovers. There are four cinemas and a video library, as well as a museum containing costumes, props, accessories, antique movie cameras, and a rich history of the film industry going back to the Lumière brothers.

<u>Hours</u>: Open Monday and Wednesday through Sunday from 12 noon to 7 pm. Closed Tuesday.

<u>Admission</u>: Adults 10 €, under age 18, 5 €. Free audioguide with admission. Covered by the Museum Pass.

<u>Getting there</u>: Take the Metro line 6 to Bercy. Exit and turn left down Avenue de Bercy. It is at number 51.

Promenade Plantée Also known as the Coulée Verte. Once a train track, this 2-mile-long wooded walking/jogging path runs along an old viaduct and Avenue Daumesnil. It starts at Place de la Bastille behind the Rue de Lyon sortie of the Métro Bastille and goes eastward all the way to and beyond the péripherique to the town of St. Mandé. Along the way you'll pass close by the small but lovely Jardin de Reuilly, which sits like a large bowl of grass with a walking bridge suspended overhead and smaller seating areas scattered along the upper levels.

<u>Getting there</u>: you can pick up the Promenade Plantée at either Bastille or Daumesnil, or walk to it from Métro line 6, Montgallet, which is also a nice area to stroll around and eat.

My Favorites in the 12th

Bercy Park and Bercy Village. I *never* get tired of going there. Really.

Walking in the 12th! I also love just walking all over the place in the 12th (especially Daumesnil and Montgallet), since there are tall trees everywhere and wide sidewalks perfect for strolling, Saturday open markets and Parisian life happening all around.

The Parc Floral is a great hangout if you want a change and a relaxing afternoon. What a peaceful way to re-center and dwell amidst natural beauty. It's a bit off the beaten track, but if you need a peaceful moment and you love plants and flowers, or maybe you love jazz and want to partake of the annual jazz festival, this is your place.

Paris 13th

Are you ready for yet another complete personality change from the previous districts you've seen so far? Paris has so much variety, that is why there is something to see in each corner. The 13th is known for Chinatown, among other things. Yes, there are several Chinese areas in Paris, but this is the biggest by far. It's also a district where you see a lot of high-rise apartment buildings, which builders got away with because the 13th is on the southern edge of Paris. The ultra-modern architecture of residential towers and the national library share the district with cute rows of attached private homes and winding cobbled streets. As you exit the Métro at Place d'Italie, you'll be in the center of things, in front of an enormous mall. You can shop there at one of the many chain stores and buy provisions at the Carrefour grocery store, or simply wander down either side of the shopping center into the neighborhoods.

Main Sights in the 13th

Chinatown Chinatown runs straight up and down Avenue du Choisy. It is also called the Asian quarter (Quartier Asiatique) Little Asia (Le Petit Asie), and Le Triangle de Choisy, describing the boundaries of this neighborhood. The triangle consists of Avenue de Choisy, Avenue d'Ivry and Boulevard Masséna. This area contains the largest Asian community in Paris and in all Europe, with over 50,000 Chinese, Vietnamese, and Laotians. You'll see many restaurants, gift shops, real estate agencies, hair salons, clothing stores—all with Chinese signs, and a large Asian grocery store, Tang Frères (Tang Brothers), who distribute to smaller shops all around Paris. If you are in Paris in January or February, you can see the legendary Chinese New Year parade. The dates change each year, so find out this year's date online.

Butte aux Cailles and Rue des Cinq-Diamants neighborhood (See Neighborhood wandering later on for a nice walking tour of the 13th). This area really has a village feel, so contrary to the residential towers that are a frequent sight in this part of the city. Restaurants and nightlife flourish here as well. This area used to be a farm and later was covered by windmills. It attracts artists, intellectuals, and students, and it's great for walking.

Worth Seeing in the 13th

Manufacture des Gobelins In the present day, this is a museum, but in 1662 this building was the royal tapestry manufacturer. Prior to that it belonged to Joseph Gobelin, who used it as a workshop for dyeing fabric. You can tour the museum (covered by the Museum Pass) and see 17th century weaving techniques. There are special exhibits throughout the year. Open 11-6 daily.

Admission: Self-guided visit, 8 €. One-hour guided visits, 12 €; Online combination tickets (guided visit and access to the museum), 15.50 €. Their website is confusing, so reserve guided visits by email: visites@cultival.fr or phone 33 (0) 8 25 05 44 05.

Getting there: Métro line 7 Gobelins. 42 Avenue des Gobelins.
www.mobiliernational.culture.gouv.fr/en/home

Bibliothèque François Mitterrand This is the French National Library, which contains over 10 million volumes (yes, you read it right.) Although the current high-rise library buildings were completed in 1996, this library has existed since 1368, when the first documents were preserved by Charles V. It serves as a repository of every volume published in France since the 16th century. From a design perspective, the outside of the building is just as interesting as the inside. Four enormous towers are connected by wide wooden planks on the ground, with landscaping interspersed. The whole structure surrounds a sunken woodland. It's not accessible, but you can see it from inside the building. This is not one of the many libraries of Paris that are free to join, but you can go in and look around for free.

Getting there: Métro line 14 Bibliothèque François Mitterand and Métro line 6 Quai de la Gare.

Chez Gladines A Basque restaurant full of local color. Inexpensive and large portions which may include some rowdy company, primarily students and locals 30 rue des 5 Diamants. Open every day. Phone: (33) 01 45 80 70 10.

My Favorites in the 13th

Walking, *of course*! That really is the best thing here. Don't let those huge high-rise buildings throw you off.

There are many lovely areas all over this district that will make you think you are in a village somewhere. Here is one of them:

A Neighborhood Wandering in the 13th

1. Start at the place d'Italie. Take the Métro to Place d'Italie on any one of Métro lines 5, 6, or 7.

2. Go west to Boulevard Auguste Blanqui. Turn left on Rue des 5 Diamants.

3. Continue as it becomes Rue de l'Esperance. Turn around and go to where the street changed names and bear right. This is the Butte aux Cailles, quaint and worth seeing.

4. At the end of Butte aux Cailles is the Place Paul Verlaine. Turn right on Rue du Moulin des Près. Continue on this road till you reach Rue de Tolbiac. Cross over and veer right to Rue des Peupliers to the Place de L'Abbé Henocque. Circle around, appreciating the shady beauty of the houses surrounding this calm roundabout. Then take one of the roads, Rue Henri Pape, then an immediate right to Rue Dieulafoy, where you will see townhouses in a row, a rare sight in Paris. Feel free to wander along the narrow streets in this residential area, away from the noisy crowds of Tourist Paris.

5. After that keep heading south until you hit Rue Tuffier, which turns quickly into Rue Tage. As you keep going east on this road, it changes again to Rue Caillaux. This should lead you to Avenue de Choisy, one of the 3 legs of the Chinatown triangle. If you'd like to wander into Chinatown, go left on Avenue de Choisy. Just wander until you'd like to leave Chinatown and see something else!

6. If you are now on Avenue de Choisy, you are headed back to where you started at the Métro Place d'Italie. This is the upper "point" of the triangle. If you don't want to go that far, you will see the Métro Tolbiac on the line 7, on Tolbiac (left from Avenue de Choisy.)

7. You can take this one stop to the Place d'Italie, change to line 6 and go 3 stops to the Quai de la Gare, if you'd like to see the Bibliothèque Francois Mitterand. The National Library is interesting to see, even just from the outside. The river runs along its eastern edge and gives an easy jumping off spot (and a footbridge over the river) to Bercy, if you haven't been there yet.

8. Otherwise, to see a last bit of the 13th, you can continue south a couple blocks from the library to an area known as Paris Rive Gauche, close to the Austerlitz train tracks and the péripherique to the

south. This neighborhood resembles New York more than Paris, with wide avenues and a different feeling in the air, especially on Avenue de France. In this area the city of Paris made a planned effort to city move a hub here by building companies, apartments, and transportation. Many architects were called into the task as the project was conceived and continues to evolve. It attracts young professionals, students, and college professors.

The Southwest

Districts 14th, 15th, 7th, 16th

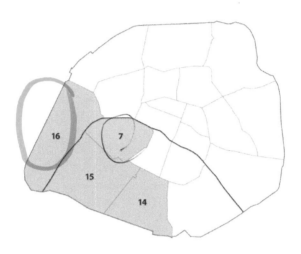

Southwest

The Southwest section of Paris includes expensive, chic, and bourgeois (7th and 16th) as well as the solid middle residential folks (14th and 15th). The entire section is respectable, attractive, and safe. You'll surely spend time in the 7th if you want to see the Eiffel Tower. In the 14th the main sight is the Tower of Montparnasse, visible across southern Paris. There are other reasons to explore here. The 15th, as far-flung as it seems, has some attractions you won't find anywhere else, and it's the largest arrondissment in Paris. We'll journey through this area, not chronologically, but geographically, starting our southwestern tour with the 14th and 15th districts.

Paris 14th

The Montparnasse neighborhood *is* the 14th, and it's here and in the 15th that the artistic journey of the impressionists continued once they left Montmartre around the turn of the 19th century. A structure that was built as a wine pavilion by Gustave Eiffel for the World's Fair of 1900 was moved to the 15th where it later became residence and studio space for artists. It was called La Ruche (the beehive) and gave haven to artists such as Chagall, Soudine, Modigliani, and Zadkine. The Expressionist artistic movement arose during this time. Today it is still used and in demand by artists. You can see it from outside at 52 rue de Dantzig.

The Main Sights in the 14th

The Tower of Montparnasse (La Tour de Montparnasse) Montparnasse is the name of this neighborhood in the 14th, but it is also the name of the enormous 56-story tower that dominates the skyline, the only skyscraper in Paris proper. Take the elevator all the way to the top. You'll be amazed at how quickly you arrive. On the top floor observation deck, you have a superb view of all Paris from its highest point. On the same floor at the penthouse café, *Le Ciel de Paris*, you can also have one of the best cups of hot chocolate. True, you'll shell out 8 € or so for it, but it's delicious and memorable. And just think of the view you'll have at the same time. The restaurant serves meals as well (and not as expensive as you would expect!) Breakfast on the 56th floor overlooking Paris would be quite the memory! Opens at 8:30 am.

On the observation deck you can simply indulge in a panoramic view from either inside or outside for 18 € on site, 17 € online (no chocolate, though you can buy a glass of champagne for 12 €.) Students pay 12€50 and children 4 to 11 cost 8 €. Children under 4 are free.

At the base of the tower is a large mall, with all the typical French chain stores you'd expect. If you're interested in even more shopping, look for where Rue de Renne intersects with the Boulevard Montparnasse and head north along Rue de Renne. Either side of the street has great shopping, and it's average-priced, not super-chic merchandise.

<u>Getting there</u>: see below

Gare (Train station) de Montparnasse Also near the base of the tower is the Montparnasse train station, which takes commuters out to the suburbs as well as to further points in western and southwestern France (Tours, Nantes, Bordeaux.) It opened in 1840, but in 1895 a train crashed beyond its rails and through a wall and fell to Rue de Renne outside. The station had to be rebuilt, as you'd expect. This isn't so much a tourist site, but you may need to pass through these halls at some point in your journey. There are kiosks and a lot of energy inside.

On the rooftop of the Montparnasse station is a lovely park, Le Jardin Atlantique, which follows an ocean theme in its design and colors. Most of the trains leaving Gare Montparnasse travel west, toward the Atlantic Ocean, hence the name. Next to the park is the museum of General LeClerc, the liberation of Paris, and resistance fighter Jean Moulin. This museum is a moving tribute to the people and events that contributed to the liberation of Paris from the Nazi occupation. Entrance is free.

Getting there: Take the Métro line 4, 6, 12, 13 to Montparnasse. It's a very busy area, because of the train station and so many lines going through. The park and museums are on the roof of the train station so you will access up a stairway along the inside. Follow the signs for Jardin Atlantique.

Tip: If you want to visit the Montparnasse area but are not going to the train station, you might consider getting out of the Métro one stop *before* Montparnasse and walking there, to avoid the crowds and confusion inside the station. Edgar Quinet is a good choice, and accessible to crêperies . . . continue reading!

Tower of Montparnasse

Fondation Cartier A museum of 12,000 square feet of contemporary art housed in a 6-story glass and steel office building, there's plenty for modern art enthusiasts. Its architect, Jean Nouvel, also designed the Arab World Institute and the Quai Branley Museum.

Hours: Open Wednesday to Sunday 11-8 pm; Open Tuesdays until 10 pm. Closed Mondays.

Admission: Adults 11 €; Students ages 19 to 25, 7 € 50, Seniors 65 and over, 7 € 50. Under 18 free. Guided visits in French are available but reservations are required. Info.reservations@fondation.cartier.com

Getting there: Address is 261 Raspail, 14th.
Métro line 4 Raspail, line 6 or RER B Denfert-Rochereau.

Worth Seeing in the 14th

Crêpes! You can get crêpes all over Paris and some are quite good, but authentic crêpes come from Brittany (Bretagne,) You'll find these in abundance right here in Montparnasse. Dinner crêpes are made of buckwheat (sarrasin) flour (gluten-free, by the way, unless they are mixed with regular flour for a softer crêpe. If you are allergic, be sure to ask.) Buckwheat crêpes are delicate and crisp. Dessert crêpes (froment) are made of regular flour. If you are gluten-intolerant, you can request that your dessert crêpe also be made with buckwheat. There are two specific streets and a few others scattered around this neighborhood where you can find restaurant after restaurant offering crêpes. You can hardly go wrong. The streets are Rue d'Odessa and Rue Montparnasse. Don't confuse the latter with Boulevard Montparnasse, the immense road right nearby, which also offers a huge variety of restaurants. When I want crêpes, I take the line 6 to Edgar Quinet, which touches one end of both Rue d'Odessa and Rue Montparnasse in a V. You can go up either of these roads for a good choice of crêperies. There are many other restaurants here as well. My favorites are the Crêperie de Plougastel, 47 rue de Montparnasse, and Crêperie Le Petit Morbihan at 20 Rue Odessa (both named after cities in Brittany.) I've tried other good ones on these roads.

Cemetery of Montparnasse This cemetery, the third largest in Paris, rivals Père Lachaise in the 20th for famous residents, particularly the who's who of literature, music, art, film, sculpture, and poetry. There are 35,000 people buried here and the list of notables, both French and international, is very impressive. Some examples: composer Camille Saint-Saens, author Guy de Maupassant, author Charles Baudelaire, author and feminist Simone de Beauvoir, author-philosopher Jean-

Paul Sartre, American actress Jean Seberg, and author Chaim Soutine. Entrance to the cemetery is free.

<u>Hours</u>: March to October, open Monday through Friday from 9 am to 6 pm, Saturday 8:30 to 6, and Sunday 9 am to 5:30 pm. Otherwise, Monday through Friday 8 am to 5:30 pm, Saturday 8:30 to 5:30, and Sunday 9 am to 5:30 pm.
See this link for an alphabetical list of people buried in the cemetery.
http://en.wikipedia.org/wiki/Montparnasse_Cemetery

Rue Daguerre If you're looking for a lively pedestrian street, full of restaurants, vendors, markets, and bustle, Rue Daguerre is just south of the Montparnasse Cemetery and west of Place Denfert-Rochereau. This is a huge crossroad where you can catch either the Métro or the RER B. Daguerre parallels the south side of the cemetery boundary, so it's easy to find.

Parc Montsouris This is a large public park on the southern edge of the city, designed by the same man as Butte Chaumont Park in the 19th, Jean-Charles Adolphe Alphand. He transformed an area covered by windmills and quarries into a slice of paradise in the big city. The park is cut in half by the Boulevard Jourdan, so it is bigger than it looks at first glance. There is a lovely, large manmade lake and walking paths all over the hillsides, outdoor sculptures, an observatory, and even a restaurant and a theater. It's perfect for lounging or picnics.

<u>Getting there</u>: Take the RER B to Cité Universitaire and you'll be there almost in the middle of the park.

L'Entrepot (The Warehouse) Well, it used to be a warehouse, until it became a cinema from 1975 until 1984. Then in 2003 it became what it is today, an all-under-one-roof haven for art, fun, and good food. The vision of L'Entrepot from the start was to offer a place to experience art, cinema, literature, conferences, and cuisine, comedy shows, as well as rental space for groups and conferences. Improvisational comedy sketches draw a big crowd, as do the café concerts and art expositions. You can even come for poetry and literature readings, which are free, but usually in French. Films, however, are showed in their original language with French subtitles. You can dine either inside a glass-walled veranda or on a shady patio, far from the urban noise. During the week there are daily lunch specials. (See the 20th district for a similar concept, La Bellvilloise.)

<u>Hours</u>: L'Entrepot is open daily from 9 am to midnight. The restaurant is open from Tuesday at 7 pm and Wednesday to Saturday 12 pm to 4 pm, then from 7 pm to 11 pm.

<u>Getting there</u>: 7 rue Francis-de-Pressensé, Métro line 13, Pernety.

Les Catacombes If you have a taste for the creepy, walk down stairs and through tunnels to see *millions* of skeletons dating from 1785 to 1810 This bone storage depot was once a Gallo-Roman quarry. Note: There is no restroom there and you'll have to climb over 200 steps round trip. Bring a sweater.

<u>Hours</u>: Open Tuesday through Sunday from 10 am to 8:30 pm.

<u>Admission</u>: Adults, 15 €. Ages 18 to 26, 13 €. Under 18, free. Tours available in French or English. Book on their site (significantly more expensive, but a guaranteed ticket.) catacombes.paris.fr/en More combos on website. Covered by Paris Museum Card.

<u>Getting there</u>: Métro line 4 or RER B to Denfert-Rochereau. Address: 1 Place Denfert-Rochereau.

My Favorites in the 14th

Crêpes! You should not miss them!

Neighborhood wanderings

Montsouris Park

A Short Wandering in the 14th

1. Start at RER station Denfert-Rochereau:
Some of the more fascinating and beautiful walking streets are found in the southeast part of the 14th district. As you descend Avenue René Coty from Denfert-Rochereau, bear right on Rue de la Tombe Issoire. When this road crosses Alésia the atmosphere becomes village-like for a few blocks. In this section you'll pass Villa Seurat on your left, a small street with individual attached homes where many famous artists and writers once lived and worked.

2. Keep going south and turn left on Place Henaffe. Go a couple dozen yards/ metres and look carefully on your right for a partly wooded curving street. This is Square Montsouris, more of a street than a square, with very private (and adorable) attached houses. These types of attached homes are not common in Paris, but you find them hidden here and there. Once you exit this street on the other side, you'll run right into the Parc Montsouris, a lovely large park with a lake, a small restaurant, and plenty of grassy hills where you can take your nap or have your picnic.

Paris 15th

Worth Seeing in the 15th

Parc André Citroën is a 35-acre public park on the edge of the 15th, bordered on its west side by the Seine River. It was created in 1992 on the former grounds of the Citroën automobile manufacturing plant, which had moved in 1982. The French really take their parks seriously, and this is one great example. There are 2 greenhouses and a large, flat fountain in the middle of the long rectangular space, and two groups of themed gardens.

And the coolest thing: a tethered helium balloon that you can go up into and see all over Paris at 500 feet, from Notre Dame to the Eiffel Tower. It holds 30 adults at one time. The park has several entrances and is free. Balloon rides cost 14 € for adults, 7 € for kids 3-11 years old. Free for children under 3 and Paris residents under age 12. Open at 9 am until 30 minutes before the park's closing. The balloon won't take passengers in bad weather. Call (3) 01 44 26 20 00 to see if the weather is favorable enough.

Hours: Park is open from 8 am (9 on weekends) to 9:30 pm in the summer. Shorter hours at other times.

<u>Getting there</u>: Take the Métro line 8 to the end, Ballard, or Javel-Citroën, on the line 10. Also, RER C Boulevard Victor or Javel.

Aquaboulevard This is Paris' water park, *the biggest water park in Europe*. Attached is an enormous health club called Forest Hill. It's a bit like a tropical island under a roof. There are 2 wave pools, 11 water slides, Jacuzzis, rivers, and a beach. . .complete with real sand. <u>www.aquaboulevard.fr/</u>

<u>Hours</u>: Open 9 am to 11 pm Monday thru Thursday. Fridays, 9 am to midnight. Saturdays, 8 am to midnight. Sundays and holidays, 8 am to 11 pm.

<u>Admission</u>: 35 € for adults. Children 3-11 costs 20 €. Children under 3 are not allowed.

<u>Getting there</u>: Take Métro line 8 to Ballard. This is the last stop on the line 8. The water park is at the edge of the city. You can also take line 12 or the RER C to Pont du Garigliano.

Parc des Expositions This is worth seeing if you want to go to a big house and garden show, like the annual Foire de Paris. This is the Big Place for any kind of trade show, garden and home show, book show, any kind of show you can think of. These kinds of shows are often called 'salons', like the Salon du Chocolat (yes, they have this in Paris once a year.) There are also entertainment-oriented shows, like Swan Lake. It's worth going here if they have a show on something you're passionate about since, despite the crowds, you'll an incredible variety of what you want to see. Admission varies, depending on the event. Go online to see what is happening. Click on the British flag in the upper right corner for English. www.paris-expo-portedeversailles.com

Getting there: Take the line 12 to Porte de Versailles. Then follow the crowds. The tramway also can get you there.

My Favorites in the 15th

You'll probably guess this one. I like parks, so my vote goes for the André Citroën Park. And, of course, wandering the residential neighborhoods of the 15th.

Paris 7th

If you're a tourist in Paris, you'll definitely be spending some time in the 7th. You'll be lining up with many others at notable addresses, such as the Eiffel Tower, Les Invalides, The Rodin Museum, and the Musée d'Orsay.

But that's not all, as you might guess. There are also some funky, foreign, and spooky things to see, like the Musée du Quai Branly and the Sewer Tour, just to include out-of-the-ordinary destinations. The 7th has both ends of the spectrum, something for everyone.

Main Sights in Paris 7th

The Eiffel Tower What other monument needs no identification, but instantly says "Paris"? Even a stylized outline of the tower is recognizable without words. It decorates clothing, paintings, bags, and countless other objects, symbolizing all that Paris and France have represented in the past and present. Of course, you'll have to go if you haven't already been. Don't let the crowds or the heights deter you.

The Eiffel Tower is the most-visited, non-free monument in the world. It was built by Gustave Eiffel in 1889 for the World's Fair. The Tower was scheduled to be dismantled in 1909, since Eiffel had a permit for 20 years, but this never (fortunately) happened. It was used for numerous physics and meteorological experiments before it became the world magnet for tourists. It is the tallest structure in Paris, standing over 1000 feet tall. There are 3 levels, all open to the public. The first two are accessible by either elevator or stairs, and the third accessible only by elevator. (Prices reflect that difference. Climbing the stairs is a bargain if you can do it.)

Wherever you are standing when you see it, whether from a far-off bridge or right next door at Place du Trocadéro in the 16th, it's impressive. You'll see the most stunning sight at night when the tower lights up. It's especially impressive up close, but you can also see it from many locations in the city. Surrounding the tower is long grassy park, le Parc du Champs de Mars (perfect for a picnic dinner), and across the Seine River you can enjoy the sounds of a large fountain as you observe the energy of the area and the awe-inspiring Tower by night.

<u>Hours</u>:   From 9 am to midnight, from June 15 to September 1. The rest of the year, from 9:30 am to 11 pm.

<u>Admission</u>: This reflects a price change effective January 14, 2019. There are many ways to go up the Tower!

Elevator access to top: Adults 26€80; Ages 12-24 13€40, Ages 4-11 and for the disabled 6€70. Under 4, free for all levels.
Elevator access to 2nd floor: Adults 17€10; Ages 12-24 8€60; Ages 4-11, 6.40 €.
Stairs to 2ⁿᵈ floor then elevator to top: Adults, 19.40 €, ages 12-24, 9.70 €. Ages 4-11, 4€30.
Stairway access to 2nd floor: Adults 10€70; Ages 12-24, 5€40; Ages 4-11, 2€70. <u>Stairway</u> tickets are not sold <u>online.</u> You can buy tickets or get more information online at <u>http://www.tour-eiffel.fr/en.html</u>.

<u>Getting there</u>: Take the Métro line 6 to Bir Hakim or the line 9 to Trocadéro.

La Tour Eiffel

Musee d'Orsay is home to some of France's finest art treasures, and the world's largest collection of impressionist and neo-impressionist art. The gorgeous building is a former train station in the ornate neoclassical architectural style. Many people who don't know art still likely know the names Monet, Van Gogh, Renoir, Degas, and Cezanne. Most of the works here are from 1848 to 1915. In 1970 the train station, La Gare d'Orsay, was about to be torn down, when instead it was named an historic place and given special protection. It was finally opened as a museum in 1986 by the president at the time, François Mitterand. Here you can see Van Gogh's Starry Night and Monet's Blue Water Lilies, among many other breathtaking works.

For more info see the official web site: www.musee-orsay.fr/en/

<u>Hours</u>: Open Tuesday, Wednesday, and Friday through Sunday from 9:30 am to 6 pm and on Thursdays from 9:30 am to 9:45 pm. Closed Mondays.

<u>Admission</u>: 16 € for adults. This includes both permanent collections and temporary exhibits. Under 18 free. 13 € for those ages 18-25 from non E.U. countries; free for those 18-25 from E. U. countries. Free the first Sunday of the month. Reduced prices daily after 4:30 pm except Thursday, after 6 pm. Included in the Museum Pass.

<u>Getting there</u>: Métro line 12 Solférino, or RER C Musée d'Orsay.

MEDIEVAL WEAPONS

Les Invalides What is that gold-domed building that you can see from all over central Paris? It is Les Invalides, currently a military museum. Whether you're a military buff or not, you may be interested to know that Napoleon is buried here, as are many other French military heros. You won't know some of them, unless you are French, but it's a fascinating history lesson! Napoleon had been in exile since 1815 when he died in 1821. He was buried where he lived in exile, on the island of Saint Helena. Years later, in 1840, on the orders of King Louis-Philippe, Napoleon's coffin was brought to Paris, and he was given a belated state funeral, with much pomp and ceremony.

This structure is more than a museum. It's also a monument, a hospital, and a home for retired veterans.

Built in 1671, its architectural style is baroque, with all the ornate glitz popular in that period. Louis XIV began the project as a hospital for war wounded and retired soldiers, hence the name Les Invalides, and included a lovely chapel. A century later, an angry mob stormed Les Invalides for arms stored there, stealing cannons and muskets to start a revolution. From there they went to the Bastille prison and the French Revolution was born.

Come see weapons and armor from the 14th to the 18th century. The Medieval Room displays arms from the 13th to 15th centuries. The Royal Room contains exquisite and ornate arms used by kings and nobility. There are also classical concerts offered throughout the year at an extra charge. See their website for additional information. http://www.musee-armee.fr/en/english-version.html

Hours: Les Invalides is open daily from 10 am to 6 pm, and until 9 pm on Tuesdays. Closed January 1, May 1, and December 25.

Admission: 14 € for Adults for the museum and the exhibits, both temporary and permanent, including Napoleon's tomb. Free for those under age 18. Free to age 25 for European residents. All others, 11 €. Covered by the Museum Pass. Group rates available. (Order tickets online at a higher rate.)

Getting there: Métro line 8 Invalides; RER C Invalides.

Musée Rodin (Rodin Museum) August Rodin (1840-1917) was one of the most famous sculptors in the world, and his works, inspiring, evocative, and sometimes a bit erotic, are on display at the Rodin Museum in the 7th on 79 Rue de Varenne. You've probably seen some of his sculptures, the most famous being The Thinker and The Kiss. His work wasn't well-accepted at first because he didn't follow the conventions of his day, but with time he became known all over the world for the realism and emotion he cast into bronze. At the museum you'll see bronze works inside and out in the gardens as well. http://www.musee-rodin.fr/en

Hours: Open daily from 10 am to 6:30 pm. Closed Mondays.

Admission: 13 € for Adults. Free for children up to age 18; Reduced price (9 €) for ages 18 to 25 non-E.U. residents; Permanent exhibits and gardens are free for age 18-25 E.U. residents. From October 1 to March 31 the museum is free the first Sunday of each month. Free with the Museum Pass. Audio guides with 2 hours of content are available in French, English, and Spanish for 6 €. Guided visits are also available.

Getting there: Métro line 13 Varenne or RER C Les Invalides.

Worth Seeing in the 7th

Rue Cler There are many picturesque pedestrian streets lined with open market vendors, restaurants, and flower shops, but this one ends up in nearly every tourist book. It has been called the best market street in Paris. It could very well be true, though it may be a close competition. You'll just have to check out (and eat your way through) several of them to see which one you like best. You'll find plenty to enjoy here with patisseries, fishmongers, fruit stands, restaurants, cheese shops, and much more. It is strictly pedestrian, with original cobblestones underfoot. Prepare your picnic with its fixings, or just find a nice open-air café for your hot lunch or salad. Many shops are closed on Mondays (as nearly everywhere in France), but you should be fine on every other day.

Musée du Quai Branly If you'd like a more exotic or primitive flavor in your next museum visit, try this one, opened in 2006 to feature the cultural expressions of Asia, Africa, and elsewhere around the world. In the permanent collection you'll see over 3,500 items from tribal and aboriginal lands. That could take more than a day to see. The building itself was designed by architect Jean Nouvel, who also designed the Arab World Institute, and many other notable buildings in Paris. From late June to late September, you can access the roof for a panoramic view of all Paris (separate ticket.)

<u>Hours</u>: Open Tuesday through Sunday from 10:30 am to 7 pm and until 10 pm on Thursdays. Closed Monday.

<u>Admission</u>: Full price 10 €; temporary exhibits 10 €, combined ticket, 12 €. Children under age 18, free. E. U. residents under age 26, free. Free with the Paris Museum Pass. For those age 19-26, 7 €. Free first Sunday of month. Shows, concerts, lectures, workshops, and guided tours are also available. Audio guide, 3 €. http://www.quaibranly.fr/en

<u>Getting there</u>: 37 Quai Branley, RER C or Metro line 9 Pont de l'Alma

American Library in Paris Okay, this isn't probably the place you'd likely go on your Paris vacation, but if you happen to be in Paris for any length of time (say, you're an exchange student or a businessperson on a six-month to two-year stint) you may wish to know the whereabouts of the largest English language library in Europe. This is it, on 3 floors, despite its unimposing front facade. Membership isn't free, but it's very reasonable when you consider what you have access to every day (except Monday, as you would expect.) You can get a short-term membership (3 months) or longer, usually one year. The library holds special events, story hour (in English) for children, and a continual supply of new acquisitions. https://americanlibraryinparis.org/

Getting there: Métro line 9 to Pont de l'Alma. Cross the river and descend Avenue Rapp. Right on Rue du Général Camou. Look for # 10. Phone 01 53 59 12 60.

Paris Sewer Tours (Les Égouts) For an unusual historical angle, come see Paris from underground. Visit the underground sewer system and learn about its historical and current use, including water distribution.

Hours: Open Tuesday to Sunday from 10 am to 5 pm.

Admission: Adult admission, 9 €. Children age 6 to 16, 7€. Children under 6, free. Covered by the Museum Pass. Tours last 20-30 minutes. No reservation is required.
https://en.parisinfo.com/paris-museum-monument/71499/Musee-des-egouts-de-Paris

Getting There: Take Métro line 9 to Pont de l'Alma. Access to the Sewer Tour is facing number 93 Quai d'Orsay.

When you are at the Pont de l'Alma, you'll see a large sculpture of a golden flame. This is a memorial to the memory of Lady Diana, who died in Paris in 1997.

My Favorites in the 7th

The Eiffel Tower at night . . . gotta see it. At night there is a magic about it very different from the day.

I love the *American Library* and I spent a lot of time there. So many volumes in English at my fingertips, for research or pleasure reading.

Musée d'Orsay Exceptional visual treasures in a building that's a work of art in itself.

Paris 16th

The 16th district follows the sloping west corner of Paris. It is mostly residential and includes of some of the highest-priced real estate in the city. It is officially on the north bank but extends so far down that you might think otherwise. It's two primary claims to fame in the tourist world are: the "second half" of the Eiffel Tower area, which is the section on the other side of the Seine River, and: the renowned Bois de Boulogne, a massive, wooded area to the west with much more than a park and acres of trees, as you will see.

Main Sights in the 16th

Place du Trocadéro To complete your Eiffel Tower experience, you'll need to cross the river westward across the Pont d'Iéna. A massive semi-circular building (two buildings, actually) dominates the skyline from the hillside. In that building are several museums. To the right facing the semi-circle is the *Palais de Chaillot*. The museum inside is called the <u>Cité de l'Architecture et du Patrimoine.</u> It showcases French architecture past and present, including the monuments that illustrate France's turbulent and glorious history.

<u>Hours</u>: Every day from 11 am to 7 pm except Tuesday (closed) and Thursday (extended hours to 9 pm.) Address: 1 Place du Trocadéro et du 11 Novembre.

<u>Admission</u>: Permanent collections, 9 €. Combination tickets of temporary and permanent exhibits, 12 €. Under age 18, free. Ages 18-25 non-E.U. residents, 6 €. Age 18-25 E.U. residents, free. Holders of Museum Pass, included. Discounts exist for families (2 adults and 2 children.) Free the first Sunday of each month.

<u>Musée de l'Homme</u>: This is THE natural history museum in Paris, focused on anthropology and prehistory. In over 100,000 square feet, there are thousands of objects as well as temporary exhibits and an immense library. It is arranged geographically, covering 5 continents.

Hours: 11 am to 7 pm daily except Tuesdays (closed).
http://www.museedelhomme.fr/

Admission: Admission: Adults, 12 € for permanent and temporary exhibits; 9 € for ages 4 to 25. Full-price tickets valid for 3 months for discounts at Jardin des Plantes museums and Parc Zoologique de Paris (Zoo) and vice versa. Inquire on-site. Covered by the Museum Pass. Free under age 25 for E. U. residents.

Theatre National de Chaillot: A theatre in the same complex that is dedicated to drama and dance. For programs, see www.theatre-chaillvilletteot.fr/en. See the program online in English. Buy tickets online or at the box office Monday through Friday, 11 am to 6 pm or Saturday 2:30 pm to 6 pm. You can also get tickets from outlets like FNAC stores or through discounters like Ticketac (online).

Musée National de la Marine: Paris' maritime museum, including history, science, and human stories. There are 5 such museums mostly in coastal cities. At the time of this writing, the Paris museum is undergoing renovation. Check the website for updates. www.musee-marine.fr

Hours: Monday through Saturday, 11 to 7 pm. Saturday, 2:30 to 6, Wednesday, Thursday, Friday from 11 am to 7 pm. Closed Tuesdays.

<u>Admission</u>: 8€50 for adults. Combination ticket for permanent and temporary exhibits, 10 €. Children to age 18 are free, Age 18-26 residents of the E. U. are free. Age 18-26 from other countries, 6 €. Temporary exhibits may cost a bit more.

<u>Getting there</u>: The address is 17 Place du Trocadéro. You may already be there if you've just visited the Eiffel Tower. Otherwise, take line 6 or line 9 to Trocadéro.

Bois de Boulogne This isn't really a park as much as it is a huge forest, commissioned by Napoleon. It is the second largest park in Paris (after the Bois de Vincennes on the east side) and covers over 2,000 acres or 8.5 square kilometers. You'll find lakes and cascades, botanical gardens (Bagatelle is one, see below), greenhouses containing hundreds of thousands of plants, two horse-racing tracks, an amusement park called le Jardin d'Acclimatation (more below), and the tennis courts where the Roland Garros French open is held each year. More than just a park, eh?

<u>Jardin de Bagatelle</u>: This gorgeous park to the west of Paris was created in 1777 on a bet between Marie Antoinette and the Count d'Artois, that he couldn't create a park in 3 months. He did, in just 63 days, but it doesn't look like a rush job. When you're a count, you can get people to do things for you *pronto*. Today the park is owned by the city of Paris and is called the "Anglo-Chinese gem", following a style popular back then. Look

for themed gardens, concerts, special exhibits, a chateau, and a rose garden that has hosted international competitions annually since 1907.

Hours: The park opens at 9:30 am and is open until 8 pm in warmer months. From October to March, it closes at 6:30 pm.

Admission: From May 1 to October 31, adult admission is 2€50 for adults, 1€50 ages 7 to 26. Below age 7, free.

Getting there: It isn't direct, but worth the trip. Take the Métro line 1 to Pont de Neuilly or Porte Maillot, then catch bus # 244.

Jardin d'Acclimatation: This garden is a children's amusement park, first opened in 1860. It was fully renovated in 2018 and is full of interesting distractions likely to appeal to young'uns. Among these are a house of mirrors, a mini-golf course, a zoo, a puppet theater, rides like the log flumes and the merry-go-round, shooting galleries, an archery range, and small cars that kids can drive. http://www.jardindacclimatation.fr/ A bilingual PDF is available on their web site. There are restaurants, a picnic area, and handicap access.

Hours: Open Monday, Tuesday, Thursday, and Friday from 11 am to 6 pm. Open Wednesdays, weekends, and school holidays from 10 am to 6 pm.

<u>Admission</u> Access to the gardens: 7 € for adults and children over 3 years; free for children ages 3 and younger. 4€ for seniors and large families. Attractions are extra, normally between 1 and 3 tickets. Book of 15 tickets, 45 €. Access to gardens and all attractions, request the Pass Illimite online. This will give you unlimited access to rides. Starting at 25. Tickets must be purchased 7 days in advance to get this price. Package price changes according to the season. Attraction tickets can be purchased in single units.

<u>Getting there</u>: Take Métro line 1 to Sablon and it's a 5-minute walk from there.

The Paris Museum of Modern Art (Musée d'Art Moderne de la Ville de Paris) This is Europe's largest space for modern art, housed in the impressive Palais de Tokyo, built in the 1930s. Here you'll see many Avant-Garde works, as well as classics and impressionist paintings. Two restaurants are on site, Monsieur Bleu and Les Grands Verres. There are guided tours and workshops for adults and children, though these are done in French. For current exhibits, consult their website. www.palaisdetokyo.com/en

<u>Hours</u>: Open noon to 9 pm every day except Tuesday.

<u>Admission</u>: Adults 9 €, Children to age 18, free. 19-26, 6 €. Admission includes all exhibits and tours. Entrance to

the building is free if there are no special exhibits occurring.

<u>Getting there</u>: address is 13 Ave. du President Wilson. It is between the Champs-Elysees and the Eiffel Tower. Take Métro line 9 (Alma-Marceau or Iéna) or RER C Pont de l'Alma.

Worth Seeing in the 16th

Musée Guimet This is a fine museum of Asian art, one of the largest collections outside of Asia, with 60,000 works from China, Japan, Central Asia, Korea, India, and Egypt.

<u>Hours</u>: Open 10 am to 6 pm every day except Tuesday.

<u>Admission</u>: Combination ticket including the permanent and temporary expositions 11€50. Free under age 18 and E. U. residents ages 18 to 25. From ages 18 to 25 non-E.U. residents, 8€50. Covered by the Museum Pass. Free the first Sunday of each month. Free audio guides in 8 languages available. Any ticket purchase includes a free return visit within 14 days.

<u>Getting there</u>: Line 9 to Ièna, Line 6 to Boissière. http://www.guimet.fr/

Musée Marmottan Monet This former hunting lodge for the Duke of Valmy was opened in 1934 as a museum of impressionist and post-impressionist art. Works include those of Monet, Renoir, Degas, Morisot, Sisely, Manet, Pissaro, and Gaguin, among other illustrious names. It's a perfect impressionist complement to the Musee d'Orsay.

Hours: Open daily 10 am to 6 pm except Monday. Thursdays open until 9 pm.

Admission: 12 €; Free for children under 7. For those between ages 8 and 18 or students up to age 25, 8€50. Audio guides available for 3 €. (Lasts one and a half hours.)

Getting there : 2 Louis Boilly ; Metro line 9, La Muette telephone : +33 1 44 96 50 33.

Musée de Vin Discover the history of wine in France with a self-guided tour, accompanied by a helpful audio guide. As you walk through the vaulted cave-like space you'll see many displays of wine-making tools and artifacts used over the centuries. A restaurant on site is available for lunch.

The museum also provides wine tastings, wine courses, and special dinners that follow regional themes, and include 3 wines from the highlighted region, with informational commentary about them. Reservations are required for classes and dinners (by website or phone.) www.museeduvinparis.com Phone: 01 45 25 63 26.

Hours: Museum hours are Tuesday through Friday from 10 am to 4:30 pm. And Saturdays from 10 am to 6 pm. The restaurant (Les Echansons) is open from Tuesday to Saturday from 12 to 3 pm. Tastings take about 2 hours and can be morning or afternoon. The schedule changes so it's best to consult the website.

Admission: Admission to the museum is 12€50. Access plus a glass of wine is 15€50. Three different wines with a 20-minute commentary from the sommelier, 40€. A 2-hour tasting course including five wines is 65 € per person. Themed wine dinners, consult the website for times and prices. Currently, reservations are required for all visits. Times slots are on their website. Reservations: info@museeduvinparis.com. museeduvinparis.com

Getting there: Address is 5, Square Charles Dickens, a tiny road next to Rue des Eaux. It is very close to the Metro stop Passy. Take line 6 to get there, or RER C to Champ de Mars-Tour Eiffel.

My Favorites in the 16th

Musée Marmottan Monet it's not as famous among tourists as the Musée d'Orsay, but it houses more Monet works than any other museum. If you like impressionist art, this is your place.

Place du Trocadéro I like the energy here, as well as the people-watching. Of course, you'll want to come in the evening when the Eiffel Tower is lit up. You can picnic at its feet on the grounds or listen to fountains filling the air with their music.

The Northwest
Districts 8th, 2nd, 9th, 17th

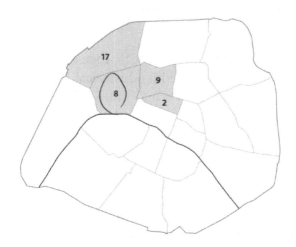

Northwest

From the must-see tourist spots of the 8th to the quiet residential streets of the 17th, you'll appreciate the change. And there's still plenty to see. As with the other quadrants, variety and beauty abound and there's something for everyone. Cruise along the crowds of people jamming the wide avenues of the Champs-Elysées, right up to the Arc de Triomphe in the 8th. Gawk at the opulent Opéra Garnier or go shopping in the 9th at one of the flagship "grands magasins" of Paris, such as the Galeries Lafayette or Printemps.

Then there's the hidden charm and quiet streets of the 2nd and 17th districts. There, you'll transition from tourist Paris to life Pris.

We'll start our tour in the glitzy 8th, then move to quieter streets of the 2nd, with hidden historical "galeries", the shopping frenzy of the 9th, and finish off in the out-of-the-way 17th neighborhoods.

Main Sights of the 8th

Champs-Elysées is one of the most famous avenues in the world. In Paris it is THE place to stroll and shop on wide, crowded sidewalks. The street extends just over a mile from the Place de la Concorde, with the noteworthy obelisk (a gift from Egypt) to the Arc of Triumph, where 12 roads enter a roundabout surrounding the monument.

During the Second World War German troops marched down the Champs-Elysées in 1940 when France fell to German occupation. French and Allied troops marched on this same avenue in 1944 when France was liberated. Aside from a lot of history, you will see many stores, restaurants, and cafés. This area tends toward pricey for restaurants, though some simple fare is available. Many shops are branches of chain stores you'd see in any mall (H & M, Sephora, Monoprix, Gap, Disney), alongside the very chic and exclusive boutiques such as Guerlain, Louis Vuitton, and Cartier. Several large movie theatres (Gaumont and UGC) have a presence here, as well as Lido, a cabaret in operation since 1946. You'll also find well-known theaters for stage plays or comedy routines on nearby cross-streets.

There is quite a bit of nightlife on or near the Champs-Elysées. You can wander around and find many nightclubs, bars, cabarets, movie theatres, stage theatres, restaurants, and much more.

Each year between November and January, Christmas lights on the trees line either side with color. In December the annual Christmas Market (Marché de Noël) takes up residence in small, whitewashed booths, about halfway between the Concord and the Arc of Triumph. If you're in Paris on New Year's Eve or on July 14th (Bastille Day, anniversary of the French Revolution), fireworks will be on the schedule, and also on the 14th, there is a large military parade with the president himself on site for the event. Be ready for record crowds at both events. The presidential palace is nearby, though not on the Champs itself. It is called L'Elysées.

Getting there: The Métro line 1 serves several stops along the Champs-Elysées, starting with Concord, then continuing in a line to Champs-Elysées Clemenceau,

Franklin D. Roosevelt, George V, and Charles-de-Gaulle Etoile (where you find the Arc of Triumph). This final stop is also served by the RER A (red line). The word "étoile" means star and refers to the formation of 12 roads joining together, resembling a star.

Arc de Triomphe (Arc of Triumph) This world-famous monument sits at the west end of the Champs-Elysées forming an appropriately dramatic end point of this world-renowned avenue. Built between 1806 and 1836, the monument was initiated by Napoleon to honor those who fought in the wars during his reign, and there were many. He was unable to finish the monument since he was exiled before its completion, but it was finished by King Louis Philippe, between 1833 and 1836. At the base of the monument is the tomb of the unknown soldier from World War I, where a flame is rekindled each evening at 6:30 pm.

Hours: You can visit the top of the Arc de Triomphe from 10 am to 10:30 pm.

Admission: 13 € to go inside and climb up to the top (284 steps). Students 18-25 cost 9 €. Free for visitors under 18 and EU residents up to age 26. Covered by the museum pass; free first Sunday of each month October through March.

Tip: If you want to go and look at the monument but not go to the top, there is no charge. There are 12 streets surrounding the monument. Don't try to cross over this maze of streets, since you may not make it in one piece. Use one of the two underground pedestrian passageways on Avenue de la Grande Armée, by way of the Wagram Street exit of the Métro, and the Champs-Elysées.

Getting there: Take RER A Charles de Gaulle Etoile, or the line 1, with the same name. (33) 01 55 37 73 77 www.monuments-nationaux.fr

Arc de Triomphe

Petit Palais This gorgeous building's French name is Le Petit Palais des Beaux Arts de la Ville de Paris, or Fine Arts Museum of Paris. It was built in 1900 and houses medieval and renaissance paintings, drawings, and sculptures, including such notable artists as Rembrandt and Rubens, along with impressionist artists Monet, Sisely, and Cézanne. The building itself is worth seeing, lovely both inside and out, created in the Beaux Art style of the early 1900s. There are always special expositions with limited dates. These are available on the web site http://www.petitpalais.paris.fr/en.

Hours: It is open Tuesday to Sunday from 10 am to 6 pm.

Admission: Free admission for permanent collections. Temporary exhibits are 11-14 € for adults, depending on the exhibit. Students ages 18 to 25 start at 9€. Special conferences and combination passes are available. Sometimes the lines can be long for special exhibits. Tickets can be purchased online. (You can purchase "coupe-file" tickets for a bit more, which enables you to avoid lines.) The Petit Palais is right across the street from the Grand Palais, below.

Getting there: Take Métro line 1 to Champs-Elysées Clemenceau.

Grand Palais Is an exhibition hall and a museum, most notable because of the largest glass ceiling in Europe, shaped like a large H. It was designed by Charles Girault and built in the same style and at the same time as the Petit Palais, but is much bigger, as you would probably guess by the name. Both are architectural wonders worth seeing. In the west wing there is a science museum, Palais de la Découverte. There are temporary art exhibits held regularly. The building holds events as well, such as Chanel fashion shows, important international art exhibits, cultural happenings, and other events. It also has a restaurant and a police station. http://www.grandpalais.fr/en

Hours: Open 10 am to 8 pm.

Admission: Museum entrance (permanent exhibits) is free. Temporary exhibits cost 14 €50 for adults and 11€ for ages 6 to 18. Under 6, free.

Getting there: Take Métro line 1 to Champs-Elysées Clemenceau.

Worth Seeing in the 8th

Parc Monceau It is a charming and expansive 20-acre park in the 8th. It used to be double its present size, but after the Revolution, parts of it were sold off to build luxury townhouses. (Times don't change, do they?) The entrance is well marked by an 18th century rotunda. Once inside, you're in another world. Wide gravel paths surround the hillsides where you can picnic or sit on park benches under trees. There's a small Egyptian pyramid, Corinthian pillars, a Dutch windmill, and a water lily garden, but the general design is otherwise that of an English garden. There are many statues of notable personalities such as Frederic Chopin and Guy de Maupassant. Getting in is easy and free, with nine entrances in all, and the park is open from dawn to dusk.

For a peaceful getaway (though it can get crowded sometimes) come relax in the park and why not bring a picnic?

Getting there: Take Métro line 2 Monceau.

Musée Jacquemart-André Located at 158 Boulevard Haussman, this museum was the private collection of Edouard André and his wife Nélie Jacquemart and is held in what was their 19th century private home. At their death they gave the house and its contents to the Institut de France to be a museum. While the house itself is striking, the collections of Italian and French art are especially impressive. On the ground floor is a Salon de Thé, a tea and pastry shop that deserves a serious and hungry visit.

Hours: Open every day from 10 am to 6 pm, except on Monday, when it closes at 8:30 pm during special exhibits. The café is open from Monday to Friday, 11:45 am to 6 pm and on Saturdays from 11 am. Brunch is served on Sunday from 11 am to 2:30 pm. It also is open late Mondays until 8:30 during special exhibits.
http://musee-jacquemart-andre.com/en/home

Admission: For combination permanent and temporary exhibits, Adults 15 € and 9€50 for children ages 7 to 25, the unemployed, and students. Children under 7 are free. Permanent collection, 12 € for adults, 7€50 for ages 7 to

17. Family package: Two adults and two children (ages 7 to 17), 43 €. Audio guide, 3 €.

Getting there: Métro line 9 and 13 St. Augustin or Miromesnil, line 9 St. Philippe du Roule, or RER A Charles-de-Gaulle Etoile.

Musée Nissim de Camondo and Le Musée des Arts Decoratifs Visit what was once the private mansion of a successful 20th century banker, Moise de Camondo, and see how a wealthy family lived in the 19th century in Paris. He had this house built in view of showcasing his private art collection. The cabinets and furniture are as much works of art as the paintings and sculptures themselves. He bequeathed the museum to Les Arts Decoratifs in the memory of his son, Nissim, who died fighting in World War I. These two museums are related but located in two different districts. Admissions info and locations for both are below.

Musée des Arts Decoratifs (located in the first district) is a much larger museum, also related to decoration, including textile, fashion, prints, furniture, and objects. There is also a library on site. This museum contains a large collection (150,000) of pieces emerging from the Middle Ages to contemporary styles. One can also view aspects of techniques for working with wood, ceramic, leather, metal, straw, and beads. It includes the Musée de la Mode et du Textile, covering centuries of fashion and accessories, from the third century to the present. It is the world's largest textile exhibition space. There are two special exhibits per year. If you are interested in fashion and decorative creation over the years, these two museums are just for you.

But textile isn't all you will find here. There are posters (about 50,000 of them) and examples of graphic design from the 18th century to the present day. A library and documents section houses over 150,000 rare documents, photos, and engravings. The library is used by researchers, students, and historians from around the world.

<u>Hours</u>: *Nissim de Camondo* is open Wednesday through Sunday 10 am to 5:30 pm.
Les Arts Decoratifs is open Tuesday through Sunday from 11 to 6 pm for permanent exhibits. For temporary exhibits, open Tuesday, Wednesday, and Friday from 11 am to 6 pm, and weekends from 11 am to 8 pm.

<u>Admission</u>: These museums are part of a group of 3 museums dealing with decoration and art. You can go to just one or get a combination ticket.
The *Nissim de Camondo* Museum is 12 € including an audio guide. Under age 26, free. Covered by the Museum Pass.
Les Arts Decoratifs alone costs 14 €. A combination ticket for the two museums is 20 € and a ticket is valid for 4 days. Under age 26, free.
https://madparis.fr/

<u>Getting there</u>: Nissim de Camondo: 63 rue Monceau. Métro line 2 Monceau, lines 2 and 3, Villiers.

Les Arts Decoratifs Museum is located in the west wing of the Louvre Museum, (although it is a separate museum.) Address : 107 Rue de Rivoli (1st district), Métro line 1, Palais-Royal-Musée du Louvre or Tuileries. Also line 7, Pyramides.

My Favorites in the 8th

I enjoy strolling the ***Champs-Elysées on a beautiful day***, and it's lovely at Christmas, when the avenue is lit up all the way from Place de la Concorde to the Arc de Triomphe.

I love the ***Parc Monceau.*** I try to avoid going there on weekends, when it's very crowded.

Paris 2nd

The second arrondissment of Paris is one of the smallest in the city and characterized by finance and knowledge. For example, the French stock exchange, called La Bourse, is located here. La Bibliothèque Nationale, which is the original national library (there is a more recent one in the 13th), is here as well. Though they aren't tourist spots, they're interesting, as well residential and calm. Here you'll find the *galeries* or 19th century passages that were like the first malls of France. Perhaps you've already seen some of these in the 1st district. Here in the second, you'll find a few more.

Worth Seeing in the 2nd

Passage Vivienne   To visit two lovely glass-roofed passageways, as well as the chic and unique shopping within, locate Rue Vivienne, which touches the east side of the national library, La Bibliothèque Nationale. At the end of this road is the Bourse station on Métro line 3. They are not far from the Palais Royale in the 1st, where the Galérie Véro Dodat is, in case you'd like to hit them all on the same day. The 1st and 2nd districts touch. Rue Vivienne runs along the east side of the Bibliothèque Nationale. Find where the Rue Vivienne joins the Rue des Petits Champs and go east a few paces to find the Passage Vivienne. The main entrance is at 4 Rue des Petits-Champs. It looks like a simple storefront and doorway in one of the normal buildings on the street, so be careful not to miss it. This is one of the prettiest passageways, with glass vaulted ceilings overhead and mosaic tile on the floor, with all the charm of the 19th century. Stroll through for a calm but elegant view of 19th century architecture and decor. While you're there, check out the bistro, Bistrot Vivienne, which has upstairs dining.

About four streets to the west on Rue des Petits Champs you'll find the <u>Passage Choiseul</u>. Built in 1825, its entrance resembles an elegant doorway. Don't be fooled, go inside. Here you'll find a small theatre, bookstore, art galleries and other interesting boutiques. This is the longest of all the covered passages in Paris.

Getting there: It's not far from Passage Vivienne if you'd like to see them consecutively. Otherwise, Métro line 3, Quatre Septembre or line 7 and 14, Pyramides. Entrance is on Rue Dalayrac.

Palais de la Bourse This is the French stock exchange. Though you cannot go inside (conference and meeting space is available for rent), you may enjoy the architecture, like a gigantic Roman temple with Corinthian columns all around and a vaulted central chamber. It was commissioned by Napoleon and built in 1808, and later embellished by another architect. It served as France's primary stock exchange for a century and a half. Nowadays, electronic methods have replaced many of the former ones, and meeting space is one of its primary functions. The structure is also known as Palais Brogniart.

Getting there: 28 Place de la Bourse. Métro lines 8 and 9, Grands Boulevards, line 3 Bourse.

My Favorites in the 2nd

I enjoy wandering around the streets and the ***Passage Vivienne***. It's one of the prettiest *galeries* I've seen.

Paris 9th

The main event here is the Opéra Garnier in the southwest corner, and the second most important is... shopping! Many of the large department stores and smaller boutiques cluster in this area. Printemps, the Galeries Lafayette, and many others lie just a block or two north of the Opéra. The whole area buzzes with activity with never a dull moment. Nearby is the Madeleine Church (8th), with its Greco-Roman architecture, so you won't only be shopping in this section. Then there are tea shops, restaurants, and, guess what, more shopping. By contrast, on the upper edges of this district is Pigalle, the red-light district occupying just a corner of it, and cute strollable neighborhoods occupying the rest.

Main Sights in the 9th

Opéra Garnier This world-famous opera house which seats nearly 2000 people was once called the Palais Garnier (Garnier Palace) after its architect, Charles Garnier. It was also called the Opéra de Paris and was built between 1861 and 1875. It's most often called Opéra Garnier, to distinguish it from the second Paris opera house, Opéra Bastille, built much later in 1989. The architectural style is ornate and opulent, with multi-colored marble staircase, a stunning Baroque Hall, and impressive ceiling paintings, including one done by Marc

Chagall in the main auditorium. Currently this opera house is primarily used for ballet.

This is the same opera house featured in the famous play, Phantom of the Opera by Gaston Leroux, and later popularized by Andrew Lloyd Webber in his musical. A restaurant, L'Opéra Restaurant, on the east side of the building, has inside and outside seating. You can eat there without having an opera ticket. Even if you're not attending an opera, you can see the opera house and its elegant architecture, and visit the opera museum, included in your admission.

The official web site gives program information in English for both opera houses.
https://www.operadeparis.fr/en/

Hours: 10 am to 5 pm from September to mid-July, and 10 am to 6 pm from mid-July to September, except on days of opera performances, when the opera closes to the visiting public at 1 pm.

Admission: 14 € for adult visits including temporary exhibits. 12 € for permanent exhibits. 10 € for students ages 12 to 25, or 8 € during special exhibits. Free to children under 12. Tickets are available in advance online. Admission includes the museum and library. Included in the Museum Pass.

<u>Getting there</u>: Take Métro lines 3, 7, or 8 Opéra. Also, RER A, Auber will get you there. If you drive, you can park at Galéries Lafayette. Enter parking at the corner of Rues Scribe and Auber.

Les Grands Boulevards This shopping area is nearby the Opéra Garnier and offers a variety of commercial experiences, from huge department stores to affordable boutiques and everything in between. You have chain stores, restaurants, theatres, and designer stores. A famous department store, the Galéries Lafayette, has been a fixture on the French shopping horizon for decades. It has one entire floor devoted to gourmet foods, including several types of baguettes, dozens of cheeses, and a whole aisle of mustards. Gift food at its finest (if you need a souvenir for the pickiest of your shopping list or your favorite foodie.) If you're visiting Paris around Christmas, you'll be thrilled by the light display outside the store.

<u>Getting there</u>: Take Métro line 9 Grands Boulevards; Galeries Lafayette is at 40 Boulevard Haussmann.

A close competitor to Lafayette is Printemps, just a block or two away at 64 Boulevard Haussmann. These and other stores are just north of the Opéra Garnier. Métro Chausée d'Antin or RER A Auber.

Worth Seeing in the 9th

Musée Grévin Paris' own Wax Museum. Yes, there's one here too. Come visit Marilyn Monroe, Ryan Gosling, Harrison Ford, Donald Trump, Leonardo DiCaprio, Penelope Cruz and many more. If you love wax museums, this is for you. www.grevin-paris.com

Hours: Open 7 days per week, 9:30 am to 7 pm.

Admission: For reserved tickets, Adults, 20 €. Children, ages 5 to 15, 16 €. Family ticket: 2 adults maximum, 17 € per person. Children under 5, free. Non-reserved tickets, Adults 25 €, Children 18 €50. Wednesday, kids' tickets are half-price. Combination tickets to other excursions are listed on their website. Covered by the Museum Pass.

Getting there: Métro line 9, Grands Boulevards or Richlieu Drouot. Address: 10, boulevard Montmartre

Musée de Gustave Moreau French symbolist painter (1826-1898) whose works are house in his own private home, which he arranged to be a museum of his works after his death. http://musee-moreau.fr/

Hours: Open daily except from 10 am to 6 pm. Closed Tuesday.

Admission: 7 € for adults and 5 € reduced rate for unemployed visitors for permanent exhibits. Temporary exhibits, 9 € and 7 €. Free to all under 18, or residents of the European Union under 26.

Getting there: Métro Trinité or Saint Georges (both on line 12) Téléphone : (33) 01 48 74 38 50. Address is 14, rue de La Rochefoucauld.

La Madeleine Church had its origins in 1162, though the current neoclassical church was built much later, after many revisions. Located at Place de la Madeleine.

To taste southwestern regional cuisine, try **Chez Papa**, which features specialties that region of France, including Cassoulet, a special bean and pork stew. Located at 59, Rue de Clichy (33) 01 40 35 89 01 Métro lines 2 or 13 Place de Clichy or lines 3, 12, or 13 Liège . http://www.chez-papa.com/

A Short Neighborhood Wandering in the 9th

Pigalle has long been associated with Paris' red-light district, but most of the area going southward from the Pigalle Métro stop is simply a residential, classically French neighborhood where it's fun to wander around. Near Place Saint George there are some lovely streets with cute eateries.

A bit further on is the church Notre Dame de Lorette, built between 1823 and 1836 by Louis XVIII. Both Claude

Monet and George Bizet were baptized in this church. The style is neoclassical with tall columns in front. Murals were painted onto the interior walls. The inside has a clean, beautiful style, lovely ceilings, and mural paintings in all the spaces between columns and walls.

My Favorites in the 9th

I like the ***Pigalle Wandering***, especially the little row of restaurants surrounding the Place Saint George.

I also love the architecture of the **Opéra Garnier**, and the vibrant energy surrounding the neighborhood. I like shopping there, too. There are some reasonably-priced chain clothing stores, such as Promod and Zara.

Paris 17th

After the frenzy of the 8th and 9th, you're probably ready for the quiet charm of classical Paris. The 17th isn't known for any particular tourist spots, though locals have their favorite haunts, such as the Square des Batignolles and the Rue Lévis (both below.) Already the atmosphere is calmer as you move towards the outskirts of northwest Paris and the affluent suburbs beyond. The Gare Saint Lazare is a busy station that will take commuters and travelers out of the city to points west and northwest.

The 17th district sits squarely on the northwest edge of Paris. Respectably chic suburbs such as Levallois-Perret and Asnières and extremely chic towns such as Neuilly-sur-Seine, where the former president Nicolas Sarkozy and his wife Carla Bruni live, lie just a bit further with the Seine in the middle. The Seine keeps appearing as it snakes through the large area called the Ile de France, which includes Paris and all its suburbs.

Worth Seeing in the 17th

Rue Lévis is a popular pedestrian street with plenty of local atmosphere. It's a market street too, where the pedestrian alleys come alive with merchants every day except Sunday afternoon and Monday. Near Métro Lines 2 & 3, Villiers.

Open market all week

Square des Batignolles is the largest park in the 17th, and an English-style garden covering about four acres. It lies slightly northeast of the center of the 17th and provides a green oasis in the city. This lovely Square was designed by Jean-Charles Alphand, the same creative mind behind the parks Butte Chaumont in northeast Paris, Bois de Boulogne to the west, and Parc Montsouris to the south. There is a small lake, statues, and bridges, wandering paths, as well as numerous flower arrangements and a variety of trees, some over one hundred years old.

Getting there: Métro line 13, Brochant (line 13), line 2 or 3, Villiers or 2, Rome will get you there with a short walk afterwards.

Institut Vatel Maybe you'd love to have a meal of "haute cuisine" prepared by a famous French chef, but you shy away from the cost. Don't be shy. The Institut Vatel prepares these same chefs. But because they are student chefs working under the watchful eye of their professors, you'll have the same quality meal at a fraction of the cost. You won't be disappointed. There's no menu, you'll just have to trust them. But there are many choices for dessert!

Lunch menu: Four courses. Apéritif, appetizer, main course, dessert, and half bottle of mineral water. 26 €.

Dinner menu: Five courses. Apéritif, appetizer, main course, cheese plate, and dessert. Between 42 and 54 €.

www.restaurantvatel.fr/ Check their website for occasional special offers. Reserve online. Questions: Info.paris@restaurantvatel.fr

Hours: Open Monday through Friday for lunch and dinner.   Telephone: (33) 01 42 26 26 60.

Getting there: Address is 122 rue Nollet, Métro line 13, Brochant. It's a bit out of the way on a corner of a quiet road, but worth the trip.

My Favorites in Paris 17th

You could probably guess my favorite is the **Square des Batignolles** It's simply amazing how beautiful (and magical!) Paris parks are. I hope you'll sample at least a few of them as you tour the four corners of magical Paris.

I also enjoy the bustling market atmosphere on **Rue Lévis.** You won't likely run into a lot of tourists here, since it's in the northwest corner of the city, so your visit will give you a good taste of local life.

Near Paris

To the North

Chantilly (pronounced Chon-tee-yee) is a lovely town about 30 miles northeast of Paris, accessible by train in under 45 minutes. Most of the city limits touch the surrounding forest. A lively downtown has shops and restaurants. Though the Château is several hundred years old, the town itself wasn't established until just after the Revolution. And yes, Chantilly lace and Chantilly cream were invented in this town.

Chantilly is most known for the **Château de Chantilly**, the 16th century former residence of the Condé princes. Today you can tour the Château, its lands, and water gardens. This is one of the closest châteaux to Paris and an easy day trip. The Château rivals Versailles in architectural splendor and encompasses more works of art. Inside the Château is the Musée de Condé, containing one of the oldest and largest art and document collections in France. The surrounding park and water gardens are included in the admission price.

Hours: Open daily from 10 am to 6 pm during high season (March 30 to October 27) and from 10:30 to 5 in low season (October 30 to March 29). Closed Tuesdays.

Admission: A combination pass includes the Château, the park, the gardens, and the Grandes Ecuries (stables, see below.) Tickets are available on site at the château or online. Adults: 17 €. For children ages 7 to 17, 13€50. Park and gardens only, 6 €. Audio guide and 30-minutes dressage demonstration at the stables is included in the admission. The park includes 3 gardens: French, Anglo-Chinese, and English. The Park Pass is good for one year after purchase.

Family tickets are available at 48 € for 2 adults and up to 3 children. These are only available on site at the Château ticket counter. The website is full of info about the chateau, grounds, and horse museum, as well as special equestrian shows and other events. http://www.domainedechantilly.com/en/

Living Museum of the Horse This is one of the most popular sites to visit in Chantilly (Musée du Cheval and Grandes Écuries) and it's not far from the Château. The stables were built in 1719 and could hold up to 240 horses and twice as many dogs for hunting activities. It documents the relationship between humans and horses throughout the centuries. It's also home to 26 horses, 10 ponies, 3 donkeys and a mule. Almost daily equestrian events are included in your ticket.

Hours: Open from 10:30 am to 5 pm. Closed Tuesdays.

Admission: Entrance to the Horse Museum is included in your combination pass.

The Chantilly town center, the Château, the racetrack, and the Museum of the Horse are all within walking distance from one another, along with plenty of green spaces for your picnic.

Getting there: Take the SNCF suburban train from the Gare du Nord to Chantilly, which will be marked on the black departure signs. Get off at Chantilly-Gouvieux, or the RER D getting off also at Chantilly-Gouvieux. The train ride takes under 30 minutes, but it will take about 15 minutes to walk to the Château.

By car, it takes about an hour. You can take the D316 departmental road. It will cost 4€80 in tolls.

Château of Chantilly

The Chantilly Racecourse Another notable aspect of Chantilly is its reputation as a center of horse racing and training. The racecourse, or Hippodrome de Chantilly, holds prestigious thoroughbred races and dressage events throughout the warmer months of the year. The first race was held there in 1834. There are 5 races during the racing season, including the Prix du Jockey Club in June. Chantilly has the largest racehorse training community in France. Check their website for horse shows and races, dates and rates.

Hours: Racecourse gates open at 12 noon.

Admission: During the week you can get in for 3-5 € (general entry) from Monday to Saturday if you book in advance online, and 6 € on Sunday. Otherwise, 10 €. Children under 12 are free. Specific races, like the Prix de Diane Longines or the Grands Prix, the two main races held here, will be more. Free to those under age 18 and reduced for those over 60 years old.

https://www.france-galop.com/en

High season (March 25 to November 1) Open daily 10 am to 6 pm. Grounds close at 8 pm.

Hippodrome de Chantilly address 16 avenue du Général Leclerc 60631 Chantilly   Tel. (3) 03 44 62 44 00.

Senlis While you are in the region of Chantilly, you shouldn't miss Senlis, not too far away, a medieval and historically significant town. Senlis was a royal city, home to Hugh Capet, one of the first kings of France in the 10th century. You can still see the castle remains. Another notable feature is the Gothic Senlis Cathedral and, of course, the cobbled alleyways and medieval charm. The city has been a site for French films and television series since the early 20th century.

Giverny Giverny is the former home of the famous impressionist painter, Claude Monet. It was at Giverny, about 50 miles from Paris, that he painted his famed water lilies. You can see them in the back yard of his home, which he purchased in 1890. He created the gardens that he then painted and made world-famous. He lived there until his death in 1926. In the late 19th century, many impressionist artists moved to the village to be around Monet and benefit also from the natural surroundings for their paintings.

http://fondation-monet.com/en/

Hours: Open April 1 to November 1, 9:30 to 6 pm.

Admission: 11 € for adults; 6€50 for children 7 to 12 and students. Children under age 7, free. Guided tours are available for an extra charge. Free game booklets are available at the welcome desk or by download for children ages 5-8 and 9-12 in either French or English. Combination tickets with other museums are described on the website (link above.)

<u>Getting there:</u> Take a commuter (SNCF) train to Vernon from the Gare St. Lazare. Follow the Grandes Lignes signs to get to the place where you can either buy your ticket or take the train. By car, take the A13 highway towards Rouen. Take exit 14 or exit 16 and follow signs to Vernon. This autoroute is free nearly until the end, where you'll have a small toll to pay.

Auvers-sur-Oise Only 17 miles northwest of Paris is the picturesque town where Vincent Van Gogh spent the last years of his life. Always a popular town for artists, such as Cezanne, Daubigny, and Pissaro, Van Gogh moved there for medical care from Dr. Gachet, who is the subject of some of his paintings. You can visit a small museum in the former home of Daubigny, dedicated to Van Gogh and his work, as well as Auberge Ravoux, where Van Gogh lived, and the Chateau of Auvers-sur-Oise.

To the East

Disneyland Paris Apparently the most visited attraction in Europe, Disneyland Paris, as it is currently called (original name was Eurodisney), is located in an eastern suburb of Paris, accessible by the RER A. This train goes eastward in 2 branches, so make sure you get on the one listing Marne-la-Vallee-Chessy as the endpoint, (NOT Boissy-Saint-Leger.) See the official website for details: pricing, hotel information, and to order tickets online. www.disneylandparis.com/en-us/

If you drive, you'll want to take the A4 highway toward the city of Metz. Just a note: The park is very much the same as those in California and Florida (except R2D2 speaks French), so don't expect anything drastically different.

To the South

Fontainbleau is a beautiful, classy, and bustling town about 35 miles south of Paris. It has an upscale small-town feel with plenty of shops, restaurants, and quaintness. The centerpiece of the town is the Château de Fontainbleau. Along with several reputable schools of engineering and mining, Fontainbleau is the home of INSEAD, a top-rated international business school. The city is surrounded by a large forest, great for hiking and rock climbing.

Le Château de Fontainbleau: Though its origins are medieval (and only the keep remains), the Château fits more with the Renaissance, thanks to renovations by Francois I, also responsible for many of the châteaux in the Loire Valley. The palace was a favorite home to 34 emperors and 2 French monarchs. It was continuously inhabited for seven centuries. Perhaps the best-known resident was Napoleon Bonaparte, who abdicated in this very castle before going into exile. Filled with the sumptuous furnishings you'd expect in a royal castle, there is also an impressive art collection, rivalling that of the Château of Chantilly. Many visitors find the architecture as impressive as the Château of Versailles. You'll see the Francois I Gallery, the Emperor's Throne Room, and Marie Antoinette's Turkish Boudoir, which she had built as a private getaway spot. A guided tour is preceded by a film on the creation of this unique space.

https://www.chateaudefontainebleau.fr/en/

<u>Hours</u>: April to September, open 9:30 to 6. October through March, 9:30 to 5 pm. Closed Tuesdays. Also closed January 1, May 1, and December 25.

<u>Admission</u>: Adults 26 and over 13 €, children under age 18, free. From 18-25, reduced price of 11 €. Residents of the E. U. between age 18-25, free. Half-price tickets after 5 pm. Special pricing available for families and groups. See the website or ask for rates at the desk. Viseoguide (tablet) available for 4 €. Free on the first Sunday of each month, except for during July and August. Reservations required (book online.)

<u>Getting there</u>: *By train* From the Gare de Lyon, take the TER or Transilian train in the direction of Monereau/Montargis. Get off at the Fontainbleau-Avron station. It will cost around 8 or 9 €. Paris Visit Card is accepted, as well as Navigo Decouverte. Make sure whatever ticket you get will cover 5 zones. It will take around an hour. If you want to hike in the Fontainbleau Forest on weekends and holidays, look for a special stop called Fontainbleau Fôret. *By car*, take the A6 highway

toward Lyon. Exit at Fontainbleau. Follow signs for "chateau".

Milly-la-Foret This is a smaller town near Fontainbleau. If you are traveling by car, you can do a day visit and easily see the three towns of Fontainbleau, Milly-la-Foret, and Barbizon, or for less of a rush just pick two out of three. If you have time for only one, go see Fontainbleau or head out to the forest for some boulder-climbing.

Barbizon In the 19th century, the town drew landscape painters, such as Theodore Rousseau and Jean-François Millet. Today you'll still find galleries and artistic charm in this village. It's well worth a visit if you are seeking a quaint change of pace from the big city. There are several good restaurants (from simple crêperies to gastronomic fare), shops, and galleries. It won't likely take you the whole day unless you want to linger for a while. It combines nicely with nearby Fontainbleau and/or Milly-la-Fôret.

Chartres An hour south of Paris, rising up like a castle from the plains, is the Cathedral of Chartres (Basilique Cathedral Notre Dame de Chartres), a UNESCO world heritage site since 1979. From the 4th century there has been a basilica on this spot. Today's cathedral is primarily from the 13th century when it was rebuilt following a fire in 1194. Enjoy a free one-hour concert at 4:45 on Sundays. Take a tour, climb the tower, take in the stunning Gothic beauty of one of the most famous cathedrals in Europe. Then visit the quaint Vieux Quartier (medieval town center) to eat crêpes or look around a smaller taste of history and French town life.

Getting there: You can get a train to Chartres at the Gare de Montparnasse. It takes about an hour and will cost 12 to 15 € each way (cheaper if you book in advance.) You can get a train also from Versailles Chantiers station (Versailles C.H.) Visiting the church is free, but there is a fee for climbing 300 steps up the north tower. Guided tours of the cathedral are available.

To the Southwest

The Chateau of Versailles The château is a must-see on many a tourist's list! This was where King Louis XIV moved when he wanted to escape to the suburbs. The town of Versailles is also worth seeing. The château and town together could easily fill a full-day trip if you include a visit through the streets, antique shops, and open markets of Versailles.

Come see the hall of mirrors and the grand apartments of kings and queens, as well as treasures of 18th century French art. There's more to see than just the château, as mind-boggling and impressive as it is. Surrounding the chateau are magnificent gardens, which are usually free except on weekends from April to September or when there is a fountain or light display. You may wish to visit only the gardens and not the château. On the website you can order tickets, get more information about what to see there, and get a big-picture orientation before visiting. There are many individual areas to see aside from the chateau, such as the Estate of Trianon (Petit and Grand Trianon palaces plus the Queen's Hamlet and ornamental gardens), and specials light and water shows at various times of the year. See the website for all the possibilities. http://en.chateauversailles.fr/homepage

Hours: Open from April to October Tuesday through Sunday from 9 am to 6:30 pm. November through March from 9 am to 5:30 pm.

Admission: At the time of this writing, reservations are mandatory, even for free tickets. You can do this online. Adults 18 € for the château, coach gallery, temporary exhibits, and gardens. For 20 € you can get The Passport, which is good for the entire estate (including the Estate of Trianon.) For the passport plus musical fountain show, 27 €. A 2-day Passport is also available, 25 € without the water show and 30 € with the show. Musical fountain and garden tickets range from 7€50 to 9€50. Other individual tickets are available. Château visit: Free for those under age 18 or E. U. residents under age 26. Covered by the Museum Pass. The first Sunday of each month from November to March, the Château and Trianon are free. Visits for only the park are free to everyone except during fountain or music shows. Bicycles are welcome.

In summer, Musical Fountain shows take place on weekends. Musical Garden shows, from Tuesday to Friday, and Fountain Night shows each Saturday night. Reserve tickets online.

Getting there: Take the RER C train in the direction of Versailles R. G. (Rive Gauche). The train you want will have a name starting with the letter V.

To the West

La Défense If you look out from the Eiffel Tower, you'll see a far-away cluster of skyscrapers and you might wonder if mini–New York City was transplanted there. No, it's La Défense. As you get closer, you'll see how unique a corner of Paris this is.

Businesses exist throughout Paris, but La Défense is THE business district, on a far-flung island of nearly one hundred buildings and skyscrapers to the west of Paris. The best-known architectural feature is the Arche de la Défense, which is the modern counterpart to the Arc of Triumph. If you stand under the La Défense arc, also known as La Grande Arche, you stand on a parallel line (axe historique) with the Arc de Triomphe, which is not only Napoleon's monument but a western doorway to Paris. The La Défense arc was completed in 1989 and houses government offices, and a photo exhibit area. The restaurant, Les Jardins de Joséphine, is open from 12 noon to 6:30 pm for lunch and cocktails and offers panoramic views,

180,000 employees occupy over 37 million square feet of office space in this futuristic district that looks nothing like Paris. There are 1500 corporate head offices located here, and this area contains many of Paris' highest buildings. The area was named after a statue erected in 1883 commemorating soldiers who defended the capital in Franco-Prussian war of 1870.The statue, called La Défense de Paris, was moved there after the area was established. Construction occurs in waves, but is also continuous, demonstrating various styles of contemporary architecture spanning 60 years. Along with office buildings, there are many parks, restaurants, fountains, and landscaped areas. Also scattered throughout are avant-garde art exhibits, 60 works of art from 50 artists from 14 nationalities.

La Grande Arche de la Défense

A wide-domed building, the Centre des Nouvelles Industries et Technologies, or CNIT, is the world's largest self-supporting vaulted ceiling. Inside is sparkling dignity, a lovely design housing restaurants, stores, and offices. Nearby, Le Quatre Temps is an enormous shopping mall which, at the time it was built, was the largest in Europe. Here you'll find just about everything. All around la Défense are restaurants of every stripe. There are also quite a few in the CNIT Center and in the Quatre Temps mall.

<u>Getting there</u>: Take the RER line A westward to La Défense. As you get out of the RER you'll be on the Parvis, a wide and paved open space. At one end you'll see the Grande Arche de la Défense. Feel free to wander around the glass and concrete world and feel like you're on another planet.

Saint Germain-en-Laye   If you'd love to see a medieval château but don't want to travel too far from Paris, take the RER A west to Saint Germain-en-Laye. In this wealthy suburb 12 miles outside Paris, along with tree-lined avenues and bustling commerce, you'll be awed by the Château of Saint Germain-en-Laye. Built in the 12th century, this royal château has a long and turbulent history, with many edicts and treaties signed within its walls. King Louis XIV (the sun king) was born and resided here until moving to Versailles.

Many châteaux house art collections, but in this building, you'll discover the National Museum of Archaeology, with 30,000 objects on display. The gardens and the chapel are also well worth seeing.

<u>Hours:</u> 10 am to 5 pm every day except Tuesday. The surrounding park is open daily from 8 am to 9 pm but may close earlier in winter.

<u>Admission</u>: 6 € for adults or 5 € for those ages 18 to 25. Under 18, free. Free for those under age 26 who are residents of the European Union. Free the first Sunday of each month, except for temporary expositions. Covered by the Museum Pass. Grounds are free to visit.

<u>Getting there</u>: Take the RER A west in the direction of Saint Germain. Be careful about the endpoint, as there are several branches of the westbound RER A.

For information visit the web site: <u>http://musee-archeologienationale.fr/</u>

The Path of the Impressionists (Le Chemin des Impressionists) Just 30 minutes outside of Paris you can visit the places where great impressionist painters were inspired and created their works. Enjoy the fresh air in a lovely area outside Paris along the Seine River. You'll see where masterpieces were achieved, along with a reproduction of the painting itself. 4 different itineraries to enjoy: Pissaro, Monet, Sisely, and Renoir. There are also themed boat tours available and other activities, such as concerts and bike rides. The website has complete details, but most of it is in French. The best plan is to call the office of tourism and speak to someone about current happenings. Or go there for the Impressionist walk and find out more while you're there. www.seine-saintgermain.fr/fr/nos-pepites/or-bleu/chemins-des-impressionnistes/

Hours of tourist office: High Season: (May 2 to September 30) Open Monday from 2 to 6 pm, Tuesday to Friday, 10 am to 1 pm and 2 pm to 6 pm. Saturday, 10 am to 6 pm. Sunday, 9 am to 1 pm. In low season (October 1 to May 1) open Tuesday to Friday 10:30 to 1 pm and 2 pm to 5:30 pm. Saturday 10:30 to 6 pm. Closed Sunday. Email: info@otpdi.fr

Getting there: RER A to Rueil-Malmaison or Le Pecq. I suggest either emailing the Tourist office in advance for more precise details or visiting them upon arrival. (see contact info below.)

Address: 2 Ave. des Combattants, 78160 Marly-le-Roi. Go to the town of Marly-le-Roi by way of SNCF train from St. Lazare or RER A. Phone: (33) 01 47 32 35 75.

My Favorites Outside of Paris

I like the city of Fontainbleau as well as the château. Not far away is Barbizon, which is small but charming with a village-like atmosphere.

For an unusual and futuristic experience, I recommend La Défense, which is like nothing you've ever seen. It's worth a look and easily accessible to the west of Paris on the RER A.

I also highly recommend <u>Chantilly</u>. There's a lot to see there. The style of the city is reminiscent of Fontainbleau, with a royal château in both towns, but with the additional interest of horse racing and the horse museum. It goes without saying that there are restaurants and boutiques, and it's simply a pleasure to visit.

Special Categories

This section is an alphabetical listing of special things you might look for during your stay in Paris. Many of these will have more description in the corresponding district sections throughout the book. Check the index or Table of Contents to find these. In the *things to do* category (exhibits, movies, art galleries, nightlife, etc.), you can also find up-to-date local info at l' Officiel des Spectacles at www.offi.fr/. You can get a paper copy for a few euros at newsstands each Wednesday. Online exists in English.

Antiques and vintage Try the Marché aux Puces (See listing for Flea Markets in this Special Categories section for much more detail.)

Passage de la Geôle in the town of Versailles, city center, is an antiques market.

Le Louvre des Antiquaires, across from the Louvre Museum, displays antiques on 3 floors from 250 dealers. Address: 2 Place du Palais Royal, 1st district. Open Tuesday to Sunday, 9 am to 6 pm.

Getting there: Métro line 1, Palais-Royal. Nearby is the Galeries Delalande, which specializes in nautical, science, and other unusual items. 2 Place du Palais Royal.

For a collection of many venders in one place, check out Le Villages Saint Paul in the 4th district. Métro line 1, Saint Paul, near the corner of St. Paul and Rue Charlemagne. Tuesday to Sunday 10-12 and 2-6.

In the 7th, you have Le Carré Rive Gauche, with high-end antiques from 120 different sources. http://www.carrerivegauche.com/en Look for blue flags in front of the store.

Le Village Suisse comprises 150 antique vendors on 2 ground floors of 2 apartment buildings. http://www.villagesuisse.com/ Address: 78 Ave. du Suffren, 54 Ave. de la Motte-Piquet, both in the 15th district.

Don't forget to check out *flea markets* (see flea markets in this list, called Marché aux Puces) and auction houses (such as Drouot) as well.

Temporary sidewalk sales, called Brocantes, can often include nice vintage items. Check this site for a list . paris.fr/pages/brocantes-et-vide-greniers-chiner-a-paris-18730

For used antique books, visit Georges Brassens, 104 rue Brancion, Paris 15th district.

Art Focus Galleries can be found in the 6th, 20th, Ile de la Cité (the larger of the 2 islands in the Seine), and virtually every part of Paris. Find special expositions on the websites of the many museums listed in this book.

Modern Art: Pompidou Center, 4th and 5th floors; Fondation Cartier (14th). More descriptions are found under the numbered districts. Lots of galleries all over town, but particularly in the 6th.

Home Decor: Viaduc des Arts, 12th, 2 blocks between Bastille and Gare de Lyon in a renovated 19th century railway. The focus here is on home decorating.

Open Air Art: Parc de Belleville summer weekends at upper entrance. Also, The Paris Art Market on Sundays. Over 100 artists represented, painters, sculptors, photographers, etc. At the foot of the Montparnasse Tower. Métro Montparnasse or Edgar Quinet.

Other Art collections: J. C. Martinez: Antique prints. 21 rue St. Sulpice www.jean-claude-martinez.fr

Best Picnic Spots 1) Gardens at Versailles; free if there isn't a music or fountain show. 2) Parc Floral in Vincennes, Métro Line 1 Chateau de Vincennes. From June to September, entrance is 2€50, and children under 7 are free. The rest of the year, it's free to everyone. Kids amusement area costs a bit extra. 3) Quai St Bernard in the 5th overlooks the Seine in a less touristy setting. Open-air artwork will enhance your picnic. 4) Parc Montsouris (14th) Plenty of green space surrounding a manmade lake. 5) Anywhere along the seine waterfront on either island, Ile de la Cité or Ile de Saint Louis. See parks category for additional ideas.

Boats You can cruise the Seine with several different companies, which you see sailing by at all hours. Bateaux-Mouches boards at Pont de l'Alma on the right bank (Metro Alma-Marceau.) www.bateaux-mouches.fr Cost: 14 € for adults. Children under 4 to 13 are 6 €, and under 4 are free. Lunch, brunch, and dinner cruises are also available.

Vedettes du Pont-Neuf is a similar company and offers tours of one hour, leaving about every 45 minutes from Square du Vert-Galant, which is at the western tip of the Ile de la Cité. Cost is 13 €. St. Martin Canal (with locks!) and Seine tour, 20 €. You can take a one-hour tour with commentary in several languages, or book a dinner cruise at twilight.

Batobus offers eight stops where you can get **on and off**. A one-day ticket is valid for 24 hours. 2-day tickets are available for a. The boats leave from the Port de la Bourdonnais (Métro Bir Hakim or RER C Champs de Mars Tour Eiffel.) Departures are every 20 minutes. www.Batobus.com. One-day passes are 17 €; children 3 to 15, 8 €. Two-day passes are 19 €, for children 10 €.

Canauxrama offers trips through the canals of Paris (including going through the locks) and some go outside Paris. More information on page 109.

Les Péniches- these are small parked (or moving) boats that are restaurants, bars, and night clubs. See a listing in the 1st district section of the book.

Bookstores FNAC (in les Halles, 1st) is a store for books as well as music and electronics on several floors. You can also buy tickets for various shows and concerts at their ticketron. There are books galore, mostly in French, but there is a section for other languages. For a bookstore with books only in English, try W. H. Smith on Rue de Rivoli (Métro Concorde) or Galignani, 224 Rue de Rivoli in the 1st district. Of course, there's the famous Shakespeare and Company right on the left bank across from the islands. Don't forget les bouquinists, the green metal cases hanging over the Seine, and have been for nearly a century. Rare photos, books, drawings, and sometimes tourist kitsch. For a list of English bookstores: www.timeout.com/paris/feature/shopping/english-language-bookshops

Breakfast ideas Your hotel may provide breakfast, but don't hesitate to venture out to local cafés, which may offer a better breakfast deal. Not all deals are alike, however, though many will beat your hotel's pricing for about the same thing. A French breakfast normally consists of bread items, usually baguettes and/or croissants, and a hot beverage of your choice, be it espresso (the French way), café au lait, tea, or hot chocolate. Juice is usually also included. Sometimes for a slightly higher price you can get eggs and possibly meat, though this is a non-French practice for tourists. If a hotel buffet has yogurt, cereal, meats, and cheeses as well as bread items and beverages is under 15 €, it's probably worth the price, and will save you time looking for someplace else. Another idea is to head to the local boulangerie and buy a few croissants, pain au chocolat, baguettes, chaussons aux pommes (apple pastry) or some other delicious treats.

Brunches You can find brunches by area and price range, though they are not available everywhere. They are becoming more popular in Paris, but it still may be a bit hit or miss. Some brunches are only Sundays, others happen all week. There is a wide price range, but most run between 20-30 € per person. See L'Entrepot and La Bellvilloise in this book or consult this site: http://www.timeout.com/paris/en/restaurants-cafes/best-brunches-in-paris

Budget Tips Buy fresh produce at the open market (Marché). If you look for hotels in some outlying areas of the city, that is, not in Tourist Central or near the Eiffel Tower, you'll find some better prices possibly on hotels. For example, try near Nation in the 12th. There you'll have calm, peaceful streets lined with trees, and one of the biggest transportation hubs right nearby. See the hotels listing in the Practical Information section of the book for other budget hotel ideas. Also note the many free activities in this book. You can do one of your meals as a picnic. Head into the local Monoprix or Franprix grocery store or Marché and load up on what you need. You can also have an elegant picnic by going to one of the open markets and buying a meal that has already been prepared by a local restaurant or caterer. Some ethnic grocery stores (Asian, Arabic, or African) have good deals on groceries and exotic or interesting food items, as well as basic goods.

Bus rides: Here are some bus routes that offer a good view of pleasant parts of the city. Bus # 24,29 (Gare St Lazare, Opéra Garnier, Marais & Vosges, Bastille. Side streets),30, 48, 63, 69, 72, 82 Bus information is available at information booths and posted on the walls in Métro stations. You can also find bus routes in the same brochure as the Métro and RER routes, free at all Métro stations.

Cafés There are cafes literally everywhere in Paris. Just go in one that has the atmosphere you like the best. Most will offer the same types of drinks, and have food as well. Ideas: www.cntraveler.com/gallery/best-cafes-and-coffee-shops-in-paris

Cheap lunches Grocery store fixings with baguette, street crêpes, boulangerie "menu", go to the Marché and find the Lebanese or Italian booth with already-cooked delicacies.

As for what goes in the picnic, my recommendation would be a crisp baguette (and dessert) from a boulangerie filled with cheese, tomatoes, and charcuterie (cold cuts) from either Monoprix or the local Marché. If you want to get fancy, buy your fixings from Fauchon or Le Nôtre, world-famous for elegant food and snacks. A patisserie called La Durée is well-known for their multiple flavors of macarons. Macarons are light-as-a-feather bite-size treats that look like tiny hamburgers but come in a variety of flavors like chocolate, pistachio, vanilla, as well as less traditional flavors. Find it in the 6th at 21 Rue Bonaparte or in the 8th at 75 Avenue des Champs-Elysées. Pate à choux ... what is it ? It is a special light creampuff dough filled with cream. Rue Furstenberg in the 6th...last I checked, it was all they sell. And they're good!

Churches See Worship in English

Cooking classes The Ritz-Escoffier Ecole de Gastronomie Française. Métro Concorde, Opéra, Madeleine. Classes in English. Starts at 200 €. https://www.ritzescoffier.com/en-GB

www.lacuisineparis.com Métro Hôtel de Ville. French cooking in French or English for visitors. An average class lasts 4 hours and costs 165. Many different classes available (lunch, pastry, French sauces, or kitchen skills, etc.) You must reserve in advance.

See Oliversfrance.com for a post full of additional ideas for cooking classes or full cooking vacations.

Le Foodist and La Cuisine Paris are schools which include a visit to the market and a sit-down meal. www.lefoodist.com/   www.Lacuisineparis.com

Family-friendly Jardin des Plantes (For more details see the listing in Center section, 5th district.)

National Maritime museum www.musee-marine.fr This is actually five museums, in Paris and four port cities. At the time of this writing the Paris location is closed for renovations. Check the website for news of reopening.

La Vilette expositions and planetarium (19th district.)

Parc Floral playground area (12th district.)

Paris Plage (4th and 19th.) Mid-July to Mid-August along the Seine and the Bassin de la Villette. (see districts for more description.)

Grevin Wax Museum (9th district) Along with the typical celebrities you'd expect, there's a special emphasis on notable people in French history. Jardin d'Acclimatation (16th), in the northern part of the Bois de Boulogne. Métro line 1, Sablons.

Ferris wheel A giant Ferris Wheel appears at various times of year in Paris. It used to be in the Tuileries Garden near the Louvre but more recently has moved to Place de la Concorde.

Fitness Options See also Jogging. For swimming, local pools exist in nearly every district (usually 3-5 € per entry), as well as the Josephine Baker pool, an indoor-outdoor pool in 13th which sits ON the Seine River on a barge. It has a retractable glass roof for winter and rainy weather. Port de la Gare, 21 Quai Francois Mauriac, 13th. (33) 01 56 61 96 50.

Walking, of course, everywhere. Also jogging. Try the Promenade Plantée which runs from Bastille to outside of Paris (see description of the 12th, Southeast section.)

Roller blading Fridays at 10 am for 3 hours (or less if you want to finish sooner.) Meeting place is Place Raoul Dautry in the 14th. Phone 33 (0) 1 43 36 89 81. Fitness classes are sometimes offered at the American Church.

Flea Markets In the mid-19th century the city had grown so large that large flea markets had to go outside of the city limits. Smaller ones, called *brocantes*, still exist all through the year in all parts of the city, and are occasional, not weekly.

The 2 main huge flea markets are on the northern edge and the southern edge of the city. Here you'll find everything including antiques, jewelry, silver, knick knacks, art, books, vintage clothing, and furniture.

To the north is <u>Porte St. Ouen</u>:
<u>http://www.pucesparis.com/</u> In existence since 1885, it is the 4th most visited site in France, and comprises 15

different markets in one place. There are 1700 vendors, 1400 of whom are antique dealers. The main road is Rue des Rosiers.

Hours: Sat 9-18, Sun 10-18, Monday 10-18. Reduced hours in second half of August.

Getting there: Take Métro line 4 to Porte de Clignancourt or line 13 to Garibaldi.

A smaller flea market lies to the east, at the Porte de Montreuil every Saturday and Sunday from 7 am to 7:30 pm.

Porte de Vanves: On the southwest edge of Paris, in the 14th. Ave. Marc Sangnier and Georges Lafenestre; every weekend from 7 am to 2 pm. Take the Métro Line 13 to Porte de Vanves. http://www.pucesdevanves.fr/

Fountains and Canals St. Martin Canal (northeast Paris 10th and 19th, Orcq (19th), if you love fountains (and there are SO many in Paris) here's a list in Wikipedia: http://en.wikipedia.org/wiki/List_of_fountains_in_Paris My personal favorite (so hard to choose) the Medici Fountain in the Parc de Luxembourg.

French Classes Alliance Française
(33)01 42 84 90 00 www.alliancefr.org Day or evening courses (4 or 9 hours per week). General or intensive courses also available. Call or check website for current

times and rates. Make reservations at least 6 weeks in advance. See my website, www.Oliversfrance.com for post: Studying French in France, offering many options.

Another option is the Sorbonne, which offers classes all year. www.ccfs-sorbonne.fr Prices and length of courses vary (2 to 12 weeks) check website for current dates, courses, and pricing. The Catholic Institute offers classes as well. http://bit.ly/1IDQQCi

Gluten-Free Café Pinson, 6 rue de Forez, 3rd (also vegetarian). See also www.parisbymouth.com/our-gluten-free-guide-to-paris/

Helmut Newcake (bakery) in the 10th; See also Organic and natural food category below.

Ice Cream I've mentioned Berthillion, which is probably the best-known delicious ice-cream in Paris. However, you should be aware of another flavorful competitor, Amorino (my favorite), which has multiplied all over the city (20 stores in Paris). You can now find them at Bastille, Ile Saint Louis, Rue Bucci, pedestrian roads like Daguerre and Cler, Mouffetard, in Saint Michel, to name a few. There are some other Italian Gelato places that are also good.

Jogging Jardin de Luxembourg 6th, Bois de Vincennes and Lac Daumesnil 12th, Parc Montsouris 14th. You can try the quais along the river banks, but many are cobbled and might cause injury. Promenade Plantée (also called

La Coulée Verte) 12th: Established on a railroad that was abandoned in 1969. 4.5 km (or 2.8 miles) of pedestrian walkways going from Bastille all the way eastward to the Bois de Vincennes.

Moving to France Here's a helpful web site: www.expatica.com/fr/ Books: Available through the American Church, *Bloom Where You're Planted*. Other resources for expats: *Living Abroad in France* and *Living in France Made Simple*.

Nightlife Busy spots: Rue de Lappe (11th near Bastille), Beaubourg (4th near Pompidou) and the Bastille area. Check out the Wanderlust, a cool terrace overlooking the Seine at Gare d'Austerlitz. 32 quai d'Austerlitz. They have goings-on every night of the week, sometimes movies (Mondays, Tuesdays & Fridays), sometimes hip-hop, concerts (music starts at 6 pm), dancing, even fitness activities on Saturday mornings. 13th district. Open lunch and dinner www.wanderlustparis.com

Getting there: From the Gare d'Austerlitz, cross the street going towards the river (but don't cross the bridge) and look for an odd-looking lime green building. (Inside there are 3 restaurants, a fashion school, and a couple boutiques.)

Also check out the Champs-Elysées, which has numerous nightclubs and theatres. If you want to check out a cabaret, the Lido is right on the Champs-Elysées https://www.lido.fr/en, Paradis Latin in the Latin

Quarter https://www.paradislatin.com/, and of course the Moulin Rouge (see 18th District in Northeast section.) There are large movie theatres with plenty of English-language movies (look for the letters VO if it's an American or English film.)

For more classical entertainment, there is the opera. The site www.operadeparis.com gives the schedule, prices, and reservations for both opera houses, Garnier and Opera Bastille.

The Salle Pleyel is the home of the Paris Orchestra, built in 1927. For information www.sallepleyel.fr. Phone number: (33) 01 49 52 50 50.

For a listing of entertainment options of all kinds, check l' Officiel des Spectacles, a weekly listing of what to do: www.offi.fr/. You can also get a paper copy for a few euros at newsstands every Wednesday.

Oldest Paris Monument Les Arènes de Lutèce in the 5th. These are 1st-2nd century A.D. Roman amphitheatre ruins you can see inside the park (or Square) by the same name, Métro line 7, Jussieu.

Open Markets (le Marché) Place Aligre in the 12th; Open Tuesday – Sunday 9-12 reputed to be one of the best and most reasonably priced in Paris. Produce and flowers only. No fish or meats. Also try Place Monge in the 5th on Sundays (Rue Monge), and Rue Sassure (17th) The oldest covered market in Paris is Les Enfants

Rouge, in the 3rd, small and quaint. In the 6th you have Marché Buci. Daily 9-7, In the 5th, Rue Daguerre in the 14th, daily, Les Enfant Rouges M-Sat 8 :30-7 :30 Sunday 8 :30-2 39 Rue de Bretagne, 3rd. For a whole book on open markets of Paris, check out this web site www.marjorierwilliams.com/ written by an American travel writer, Marjorie Williams, who writes frequently about Paris.

Organic Markets There are three main organic open markets in Paris, although many if not most markets will have an organic section. Look for a green sign that says BIO. One market is in the 6th, on Boulevard Raspail, Métro Rennes, each Sunday from 8:30 am to 3 pm. Then there is one further northwest, at Batignolle, between the 8th and 17th districts at Métro Rome or Place de Clichy. The Brancusi Market in the 14th each Saturday is held at Place Constantin Brancusi, Métro Gaîté (line 13). La Ferme du Perigord Noir has several locations in Paris. The most central is near the Hôtel de Ville, Place Baudoyer.

Organic Food/natural food Some names of shops, chain stores, and co-ops are Nutralia and Bio-Coop.

Parks Paris has the most fabulous parks in the world. They are not sports fields, but many are real gardens with fountains, flowers, green space for picnics, pure beauty and artistic design. A well-rounded Paris visit should include a couple of these: Butte Chaumont 19th, Parc de Bercy 12th, Montsouris 14th, Monceau 8th, Jardin de Tuileries 1st, Jardin des Plantes 5th, Jardin de Luxembourg 6th, Champs de Mars 7th, Parc André Citroën 15th. And these others can only be called forests: Bois de Vincennes 12th, Bois de Boulogne, 16th. Smaller but worthwhile: Butte Rouge 19th, Parc de Belleville, 20th, Square des Batignolles, 17th.

Passageways The first "malls", built in the late 19th century, hidden treasures called *Galeries*, 1st and 2nd arrondissments. See corresponding sections for more details and addresses.

Pedestrian Streets some of these do allow cars but are primarily tourist foot traffic. Some notable ones: Rue Cler in the 7th, Rue Montorgeuil in the 1-2nd, Rue Rosiers in the 4th, Rue Mouffetard in the 5th, Rues Huchette/Severin, de la Harpe in the 5th, Rue St. André des Arts and Rue Bucci, both in the 6th, le Pont des Arts-pedestrian bridge from 6th to 1st, Cours St. Emilion in the 12th, part of Bercy Village, and the Beaubourg area, near les Halles in the 1st. Rue Caron in the 4th is more of a quiet courtyard getaway.

Seasonal Events On June 21 Paris breaks into music on every corner with the Fête de la Musique. Free music concerts of all types (and quality levels.)

Later in the summer enjoy Paris Plage from mid-July to Mid-August, on the north banks of the 2 islands. Also, in

July is the annual film festival. Films inside and out at special pricing.

On July 14 celebrate Bastille Day (La Fête Nationale) with parades and fireworks on the Champs-Elysées. In early October Nuit Blanche provides special museum openings and shows until late at night. The Nuit des Musées in My also offers late-night free Museum hours. European Heritage Day in France is called the Journée des Patrimoine and is one or two days a year in September. Dates vary, but these are days when certain monuments that are not open to the public (such as the Elysées, the French equivalent to the White House or the French Senate building in the Luxembourg Garden) are open. Other buildings and monuments that normally charge admission are free on this day.   See https://en.parisinfo.com/discovering-paris/major-events

Shopping (average to budget)- There are many stores and boutiques on the following streets/areas: Rue de Rivoli (1st), Les Halles (underground mall and surrounding above-ground streets), Faubourg-St. Antoine near Bastille toward Métro Faidherbe in 11th, Rue Rennes starting on the boundary of the 14th and 6th up toward the 6th. Some mid-priced clothing stores for women are Promod, Zara, Camaieu, Mango, and Etam. For men, Brice and Celio for men. Monoprix, a grocery store, has household goods and attractive, quality clothing as well. You can also occasionally good clothing buys on at the open markets. Twice per year most stores have big sales, *Les Soldes*. These occur in early January and early or mid-June, and last about a month each. There you can find clothing and many other items at 50% off or more. Usually, the first week of *Les Soldes* the discounts are the smallest, but the selection is the greatest. Then the opposite occurs as you move towards the final week. If you see *2ème démarque*, that means second mark-down. You can also find bargains in the Belleville neighborhood in the 20th Chinese district. Don't forget the shopping malls as well if you want to find many options in one place. (See malls.)

Shopping (chic, designer) Check out the following streets and areas: Champs-Elysées, Rue Faubourg-St. Honoré, Avenue Montaigne, in the 8th, 6th district around St. Germain des Prés. You'll find reasonable and chic both on the Champs-Elysées. More chic and pricey stores are in the St. Germain des Prés neighborhood. Wander the 3rd district to find small specialty shops featuring upcoming new designers.

Department stores: Printemps, Galleries Lafayette, which both have several locations (see 9th), BHV and Le Bon Marché (7th) are the names to look for. BHV (where you can get nearly anything) is located near the Hôtel de Ville and Le Bon Marché is located at 24 rue de Sèvre in the 7th, Métro Sèvres-Babylone. Le Bon Marché also has a section devoted to gourmet food items.

Home goods: Viaduc des Arts, a collection of boutiques in a former railway station. Come see handwork of every variety in this immense location. 1-129 Avenue du Daumesnil in the 12th, Métro Bastille, Gare de Lyon, or Reuilly-Diderot (all accessible on line 1). Flower market: interesting things for gardens, along with flowers and plants. Place Louis-Lepine Métro line 4, Cité.

Terraces and Views Institut du Monde Arab, Tour de Montparnasse, Montmartre (in front of the Sacre Coeur Basilica), the Café Moonroof in the 5th at Gare d'Austerlitz will provide views of Paris and the Seine. And of course, the Eiffel Tower and the Arc de Triomphe. For a shorter view, try the terrace atop the Pompidou Center.

Theatre At any point in time there are between 80 and 100 plays going on somewhere in Paris. Some are big, expensive productions while others are small, local affairs tucked into tiny theatres in unexpected corners. It's not unusual to attend a play in a tiny room that seats only 20 or 30 people.

It is possible to see a play if you don't speak French. Theatre in Paris offers plays with English subtitles projected onto the screen and other language assistance. Here's their website http://www.theatreinparis.com/

You can learn what's playing and where (and for what price) by checking l' Officiel des Spectacles at https://www.offi.fr/. Sold in paper at newsstands every Wednesday.

There are ticket outlets all over the city, usually at places like FNAC (a huge superstore for books, music, and electronics), at some large supermarket chains (Carrefour, Auchan) and online. Check Ticketac and Billetreduc for reduced prices. Most of these will be in French, however. For more options in English, check out the Timeout Paris website. Many theatres in Paris do offer occasional plays or stand-up comedy in English. http://www.timeout.com/paris/feature/comedy/entert ainment-in-english

Theatre National de Chaillot: for dance and concerts. Located near the Eiffel Tower, 1 Place du Trocadéro in the 16th. (33) 01 53 65 30 00. Discount tickets for seniors and under age 24. Métro Trocadéro.

Theâtre des Champs-Elysées: Hosts national and international orchestras, opera, and ballet. 15 Ave Montaigne, 8th. Métro Alma-Marceau. 01 49 52 50 50.

http://www.theatrechampselysees.fr/en/

Tours   For in-depth tours on topics such as immigration, architecture, or the Belle Epoche, try Context Travel at the following web site: http://www.contexttravel.com/city/paris

Vegetarian La Fourmi Ailée, 8 rue du Fouarre, 4th. (33)01 43 29 40 99 restaurant and tearoom. Open noon to midnight. Café Pinson in the 3rd, 58 rue du Faubourg Poissonniere in the 10th or 3 rue du Forez in the 3rd.

Vegetarian and Vegan: Saveur Végét'Halles on 41 rue des Bourdonnais in the 1st district. Sol Semilla (Vegan only restaurant and boutique selling superfoods) 23 rue des Vinaigres, 10th district.

Walking Tours Several Walking Tours are scattered throughout the book with the heading "Neighborhood Wanderings". You'll find them in the 4th, 5th, 6th (Center), the 10th and 18th (Northeast), the 13th (Southeast), the 14th (Southwest), and the 9th (Northwest). That should keep your feet busy!

In addition, the company Discover Walks offers walks by neighborhood or theme, and some are free. Check out the choices here: http://www.discoverwalks.com/paris-walking-tours/ Walks are also offered by Viator.

Also, Paris Walks offers 2-hour guided walks daily at 10:30 am. www.paris-walks.com/ Adults 25 €, students under 21 cost 12 €, and children under 15, 10 €. They have several themed walks as well as in different areas.

Wine-lovers A popular destination for wine tasters in Paris is *O Chateau*, which offers tastings, classes, tours, and even a degree in wine! http://www.o-chateau.com/ 68 rue Jean-Jacques Rousseau, Metro Louvre-Rivoli (line 1) or Etienne Marcel (line 4). (33)01 44 73 97 80 Tastings are free with the Paris Pass.

Musée de Vin (16th) For history as well as special meals and tastings, the Wine Museum of Paris is worth a look. Details in Southwest district description.

Here are a couple more addresses for wine-lovers: http://www.wine-tasting-in-paris.com/

http://www.francetourisme.fr/wine-tasting-paris.html

Worship in English

Trinity International Church (Protestant) 58 rue Madame, 6th. Service Sunday at 3:30 pm 2nd floor (in Eglise Reformée building). www.trinityparis.com

St. Michaels Anglican Church 5 Rue Aguesseau, 8th. Services Sunday 9 :30, 11 :15 (family service) and 7 pm (contemporary). French service at 5 pm. www.saintmichaelsparis.org

American Cathedral in Paris (Episcopal) 23, Avenue George V, 8th.
Tel: (33) 01 53 23 84 00 www.amcathparis.com

American Church in Paris (All Protestant Denominations) 65, Quai d'Orsay, 7th. (33) 01 40 62 05 00 www.acparis.org

La Victoire of Paris Synagogue
www.lavictoire.org/English English, French and Hebrew. 44 rue de la Victoire, 9th (33) 45 26 95 36.

Liberal Synagogue 24, Rue Copernic, 16th Tel: (33) 01 47 04 37 27

St. Joseph's Roman Catholic Church 50, Avenue Hoche, 8th Tel: (33) 01 42 27 28 56 www.stjoeparis.org

Mosque Abu Bakr As Siddiq 39, Boulevard de Belleville, 11th Tel: (33) 01 48 06 08 46 www.masjidabubakralsiddiq.org/

INDEX

See Also Special Categories Listing, page 228

Métro Map   www.ratp.fr/en/plans-lignes

Thank you for purchasing Magical Paris. I hope it's met your expectations. If you have new suggestions to offer for future editions of Magical Paris, or if you find an error or have a question, feel free to contact me at: Info@Oliversfrance.com

K. B. Oliver

If you've enjoyed *Magical Paris*, please consider leaving a review so that others can discover it too! Thanks!

For more enchanting places to discover in France, check my website, www.Oliversfrance.com. Here you'll find some familiar places as well as some out-of-the way treasures you'd seldom see in other travel books, along with helpful posts on traveling in France.

See the next pages for important tools for your trips to France...

Real French for Travelers

Why memorize French phrases when you could learn *Real French for Travelers?* This book is what you need to learn basic French to enhance your travels and get you deeper into the culture. Short, easy-to-digest chapters and relevant dialogues and vocabulary will help you communicate in French during your trip.

- Travel-relevant vocabulary lists
- Guide for pronunciation
- Realistic sample dialogues of travel situations
- Easy to understand grammar explanations
- Practice Exercises with answer keys
- <u>Now also available as an online course! (Next page)</u>

Real French for Travelers Online Course

Discount Code: LEARNFRENCH

You can study French at your own pace with this complete online course. You'll be operational in French for your trip—in restaurants, museums, asking for directions, and much more. It's Travel French, focused on what you'll need as a traveler. (Grammar, vocab, listening.) Partial courses are available if you just want the basics.

A French Garden: The Loire Valley

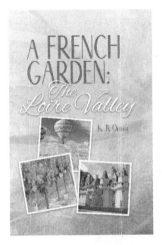

Discover castles, vineyards, and an easy pace in this stunning part of France. The Loire Valley. This concise book is the only one you'll need for a fabulous trip.

About the Author

K. B. Oliver lived in France for 13 years, primarily in Paris and its suburbs. Currently she writes fiction and nonfiction and teaches French in North Carolina. She regularly posts travel tips and suggested destinations in the France travel blog, www.Oliversfrance.com.

Made in the USA
Middletown, DE
21 August 2022

71875689R00149